Soul Guidance

Essence Rising

Soul Guidance

Essence Rising

Copyright © 2020

978-1-8382340-0-3

Published by ER Publishing in conjunction with Writersworld. This book is produced entirely in the UK.

Copy edited by Ian Large

Cover layout by Jag Lall

WRITERSWORLD

www.writersworld.co.uk

**Cover artwork and fonts by David Wyatt
at www.forgingmind.com**

Printed and bound in Great Britain by Bell & Bain Ltd - Glasgow

www.soulguidancebyessence.com

Printed in Great Britain by Bell and Bain Ltd, Glasgow

Encountering enlightenment

This book was written and compiled in the Covidian times of 2020, to assist the evolving soul on the path to enlightenment and higher consciousness.

Humanity is experiencing a mass awakening of consciousness that has never been experienced before. Souls that have chosen to incarnate at this time have chosen to be part of this evolutionary process and ascend to higher consciousness. You've been entrusted with carving new paths to embodying higher consciousness whilst in physical human form on Planet Earth, otherwise known as Ascension.

The daily wisdom that is shared in *Soul Guidance* offers humanity alternative perceptions for the reality that they live in and expands awareness and perceptions beyond current limitations. Encoded with gems that spark the soul on the journey to enlightenment and guides the soul to align with the truth of its journey in this lifetime, encompassing more light along the way. The daily affirmations assist in creating new beliefs and dissolving any ingrained subconscious patterns.

Whilst this book guides the soul on the path to enlightenment it's also activating your path and assisting your Ascension to higher consciousness. The mandala on the cover forms part of that activation and would be beneficial if used to meditate with. The mandala will be remotely updated with new keys and codes as I receive them, for you to download.

I am deeply honoured and humbled to be assisting souls on the path to Ascension in this time of great awakening. Thank you for taking the soul guidance journey on the path to Ascension.

Appreciation

Much gratitude and respect for all those who believed in me when I never believed in myself. For all those who saw me, before I was able to see myself. For the divine wisdom that comes through me and the never-ending blessings bestowed upon me. I am grateful and honoured to be here now, assisting humanity's Ascension process.

With special thanks and appreciation to my mum, dad and family, for cultivating me to be who I am. To all the ancestors, who came before me and made my life and this path possible. I salute you. I am eternally grateful.

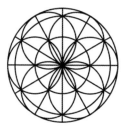

1 January

Newness is something that you create and initiate, whilst the globe celebrates the end of one Gregorian year and the beginning of another. Know that you've had numerous beginnings and endings in your own personal timeline. You make resolutions and honour them consistently. Remove the pressure of feeling that you have to comply with all the defined societal norms at this time.

Curling up under a blanket and having some me time may be just what your soul needs right now. You may want to shake off last year and go celebrating. Whatever you do, know that you are creators and initiators. You decided when to close out chapters, celebrate newness and set new trajectories. Going forward all that is required is that you comply with yourself.

Affirm

I am listening to and honouring the needs of my soul in every moment.

2 January

You have momentary opportunities to start anew and recreate yourself. When you practise momentary self-awareness you will see that every moment is an opportunity to remove or add something to your life. Whether, that's through your thoughts, feelings or actions.

Realise your powerful abilities to create and manifest the life you want. Harnessing them continuously momentarily, not just on specific days or moments. You can change direction or ideals at any moment and start energetically moving in any direction that you choose. Your physical earth experience is your playground where you get to be who you want, and have what you want, as long as you choose momentarily.

Affirm

I am a powerful creationist, creating the life I desire momentarily.

3 January

It's time to de-clutter on the physical plane. Much work is being done in the higher realms and the timeline structures are recalibrating. You'll need to recalibrate your physical life too. Being the physical component for the work in the higher dimensions. The structures that used to confine and limit you are breaking down. Likewise with your physical life. What are you holding onto that confines and limits you? Is it an object, a person, a career, a relationship or a lifestyle?

It's time to step up and be the conduit for your higher self and your higher desires. With all this clearing in the higher dimensions the physical cannot remain cluttered. Let go of what is no longer serving you and do so with confidence. Your heart and soul know the truth, listen and honour it.

Affirm

I am letting go of all that no longer serves me,
creating space for the life I truly want.

4 January

Be aware and open to the multitude of possibilities that surround you. You may have come accustomed to your life the way it is. So much so, that anything outside of it has no place in your world. If you're to evolve and grow this involves stepping out of your comfort zone and considering alternative options in every area of your life. The paths you may want to take may not be open to you at this time. However, you'll be presented with other paths that are worthy of consideration.

Use your wisdom and knowledge to decipher what is truly for you. It's time to step away from the familiar trusting in your intuition and following where your heart leads.

Affirm

Following my heart leads to the destinations my soul seeks.

5 January

You have enhanced your ability to weather the storms of life. You're well on your path to mastering the chaos and turbulence that may arrive. You're now overstanding that harmony, peace, security, safety and love are all cultivated from within. You're the source from which this energy emanates and not an external force. It's from this space that life becomes wholesome in its offerings to you.

Keep your eyes open, all three of them. Your tribe will be emerging now. The like-minded individuals who vibe on the same frequency as you. They'll feel like home and those feelings you've recently cultivated from within. Your new levels of wholesomeness are starting to be reflected in your world. It's your new vibration that is attracting your new tribe. Embrace them as love surrounds you.

Affirm

I am constantly cultivating love and peace that creates my vibration and determines my frequency.

6 January

It's imperative to release the attachment to your sprouting seeds. If you wish for your seedlings to grow into mighty oaks, your control over their growth needs to be released. They may want to grow in a very different formation than you'd hoped for or imagined. Much like the dynamics of the parent and child relations, where expectations are high and limitations vast.

You're parenting your seedlings now, love them and nurture them as you would any child. Utilise your higher consciousness to release attachments and expectations of how your seedlings should grow. Overstand that you will grow mighty oaks. They just won't be like the ones you imagined. They'll be mightier and cover terrains you would have never thought possible. Trust the natural process.

Affirm

I am happy for my seedlings to grow and cover terrains I could not have even imagined.

7 January

Become more aware of your interconnectedness with the multiverses. Every lifetime, experience and moment, has led you to where you are now and who you are now. You're connected to collective consciousness. With each moment divinely orchestrated to interface with the motherboard of all humanity combining part of the collective evolution process.

Your individual life forms part of the ascension blueprint. Continue to be a channel for the divine allowing the magic to flow through you and, to you. We've come this far collectively because you have personally. Give yourself a private party and celebrate your life, yourself and your connection to all that is. The universe applauds your achievements and so should you.

Affirm

I am a part of the collective consciousness, and I am grateful for my light.

8 January

Make changes before the changes make you. You have the power of freewill. If you're allowing circumstances, people and situations to dictate what direction your life takes, you're not utilising your power of freewill and choosing what you really want independently. When you allow your world to be solely motivated by external factors, you give your power away and negate your creationist responsibilities. Remaining loyal to choices that are not serving you will hinder your expansion.

Freewill is the gift that keeps on giving, allowing you to assert different choices in any given moment. Never fear making another choice if it doesn't work out, you can always choose again. This is your power, own it.

Affirm

I assert my free will in accordance with my
higher self and the life I desire.

9 January

Become comfortable in the uncomfortable, enhancing your ability to flow through changes. When great change is occurring in the physical world it's usually preceded by chaos, periods of uncertainty and sometimes even adversities. When the uncertainty arrives in your life know that change is imminent. You may have to lose something in order to gain something better. You may experience discomfort for a period of time and your perception about lifestyle ideals may have to change.

These are the growing pains associated with your evolvement. Learn to become accepting of whatever shows up in your world. Knowing and trusting that everything is in divine order for your highest good. Your metamorphosis awaits.

Affirm

I am safe and trust the universe to align me with my highest timeline.

10 January

Wherever you are in your ascension process is relevant to your soul's evolution and journey. You may have recognised that everyone's evolution is not at the same pace. Some souls have chosen to reach enlightenment in this lifetime and some have not. Accepting that everyone makes this choice on a soul level can be challenging in the physical realm. Especially when those closest to you, may have not yet awakened.

Trust in everyone's process like you do your own. Detach from trying to get everyone to board your train to higher consciousness. They need to find their own methods of transportation and find their own routes. Stay focused on your own path and what you're doing. You can only change yourself.

Affirm

I am accepting of the evolution of my soul and that of others.

11 January

The best way to inspire others is through example. Gone are the days of rescuing others from themselves and spending your energy on these types of projects. Your energy is better invested in yourself and your journey. Your evolutionary path has proved that you are more than capable of diminishing obstacles with your pure intentions, carving the path to your dreams. It's now time to become the wayshower. You can't rescue anyone who doesn't want to be rescued. You're wasting energy trying to hold everyone's hand and drag them down the highest path. Those around you including family may not yet be able to grasp the realms of higher consciousness and awareness, like you have.

Your evolution process and pace is unique to you. As much as you want those around you to share in the higher vibrations, you can't take any prisoners where you're going. Walk your talk and lead by example; the others will soon be following your footsteps and seeking guidance. Your expansion will be their inspiration. Focus on yourself and carving your own path.

Affirm

I teach others through the example my life creates.

12 January

Become more accepting of your own duality. As you shift into the authentic you integration of your light and dark is part of the process. Just like the joy of sharing your life with someone until they leave and you experience sorrow. Both are equal parts of the same experience. Judging these experiences, self and others' with a good or bad merit is not assisting your integration as both parts are equally relevant.

If you never knew pain, how would you know joy? If you never knew sadness, how would you know happiness? If you've never felt unloved, how would you know how love felt? This is polarity. Knowing one, allows you to know the other. Integration of your own duality is necessary for becoming whole. Perceiving experiences as completely negative obstructs the wisdom of the truth being visible. Owning and accepting the totality of your experiences good and bad will allow the wisdom to surface and your expansion to occur.

Affirm

I accept both my light and shadow, in totality.

13 January

Practise honesty, first with yourself and then with the world. You hold the power to speak your truth and need to trust your intuition. You have the ability to know what is truth and what isn't. Try not to get caught up in the finer details or desires, this will only obscure the truth even further. Truth can never be concealed in any hidden agendas.

What is it that you're currently denying? Only seeing your own agenda. What truth is it that you hide from? Be honest with yourself. Allow the truth to be revealed for what it really is and not what you want it to be. The sky is never going to be green, just like the grass will never be blue. However, you can be certain that the sun will rise and shine her light and diminish all untruths. Be that light unto yourself. Stop trying to make something be what it isn't. Only when you honour your truth will the real treasure be found.

Affirm

I accept all truths in my reality.

14 January

Surrender and trust the universe. Are you fixated on specific outcomes for current life situations? Being focused and determined on one particular outcome detaches you from universal magic. Your higher self knows what's best for you and aligns the most beneficial experiences for your evolution. This also means that you may not receive what you want, the way you want it.

Your current vantage point is limited in its ability to foresee the mapping of your life. As a multidimensional being there are several interconnected realities running concurrently that are shaping your reality momentarily. Let go of the attachment to desired outcomes and be in the flow of life. Allow your higher self to orchestrate the most magically crafted experiences, which will lead you to beautiful unimaginable outcomes.

Affirm

I am open to receiving the magic the universe has to offer.

15 January

Your faith in source energy provides you with much support. You may have never realised the potency of your connection to the universe. You may feel as though you have been quite self-reliant, not noticing that the strength of your independence is not independent of universal energies. The knowledge and experience you have accumulated serves you well, as you have learnt to trust and build relations with source and your higher self.

Your old belief systems are slipping away and replaced with the real truth of whom you are. Alignment is now, be courageous, your alchemy has created magical possibilities. You are limitless now. Rely on the powers of the universe that works with you and thorough you.

Affirm

I am divinely connected to source energy.

16 January

You have the clarity you need to harmonise your life. You have gained fresh perspectives and new insights about your life, have the confidence to utilise them for your greater good. Forming a strong relationship with your intuition entails acting upon what you feel and what insights you've received. When you choose not to honour your insights; your life will become cumbersome, until there's no other option. When you don't honour yourself, you send a message to the universe and inner child — I am not important. When you do honour yourself, you send a message to the universe and your inner child — I AM IMPORTANT.

Own your importance in the multiverses. You came to Planet Earth to be the unique vibrational imprint that you are. Your intuitive insights are original, authentic, unique and have the power to shift paradigms. The universe is encouraging confident, bold steps in alignment with your intuition.

Affirm

I honour my intuition with reflective actions.

17 January

Let go of the constant over analysis about your life. You're living out potential scenarios in your mind to the point that the actual experience has no value to you. Your mind contains much data, it's the subconscious data that you're not aware of that controls much of your life. Thinking processes can become distorted with this data that holds fear, doubts and insecurities carved from previous experiences. If you allow yourself to delve deeper into your analysis you will convince yourself that these scenarios still exist in subtle subconscious ways.

Channel your overactive mind into something creative. Don't get caught up in the illusion of fear or lack. Refocus your thoughts to the highest destination and trust that your desires can be received.

Affirm

I attract joyful high frequency experiences into my life.

18 January

Focus on your beliefs and the law of expectation. Having specific desires is not enough to bring forth manifestations. Your expectation needs to embody your desires and your beliefs, thoughts and feelings all need to align with the same energy. Have pure intentions wrapped in solid beliefs about your expectations. Now is not the time to doubt whether or not it is possible. Now is the time to know anything is possible. As a creationist your beliefs define what can enter into your world and when.

Your vortex is streaming with supportive, abundant, fertile energies. Believe in the limitless possibilities that are open to you. Inviting the magic to enter your life anyway it can.

Affirm

I expect what I want to manifest in all forms always.

19 January

Express your truth. This is time to be bold, open and expressive of what you truly want. Hiding your truth only dims your light and conflicts with your inner visions. Believing and knowing something internally requires physical behaviours which demonstrate and align with your truths. Dismissing what you believe and know to be true in order to meet expectations, fulfil circumstances and make others happy hinders your evolement.

Overstand that your truths are relevant in the world, own them and express them accordingly. Only in this expression can you actualise the true value of your authenticity and transparency.

Affirm

I honour and express myself authentically and truthfully.

20 January

Practise introspection as many events have been triggering certain thought patterns and feelings rooted in past experiences. These old beliefs have been lying dormant in the subconscious until being recently triggered by your current life experiences. Take some time out to look deep inside and decipher the truth of what is really happening versus what you believe to be happening.

Locate your own illusions and dismantle them with the power of the truth that exists now. It's time to write a new story. The old one doesn't exist anymore, unless you keep attaching to it. You can only embrace a new life if you decide to let go of the old one. The time is now to step into the authentic you.

Affirm

I dismantle my own illusionary perceptions and beliefs with the power of light and truth.

21 January

The secure feeling of home is cultivated by you. Have you been feeling as though you don't belong? This probably led you to seek out situations and people which are familiar. These situations have repetitive outcomes. What is it that you refuse to see? What truths are you currently denying? Does your perception of home limit you? Are you being suffocated by old belief systems that dictate home is unsafe, unfulfilling and unstable?

Reject the pain of the past and say no to anything that dims your light. It's time to love yourself and know that safety and security are created from within. Only then can you carve a different path, one that won't always lead you back to your original source of pain. Choose differently.

Affirm

I cultivate my own safety, security and love.

22 January

Enjoy your life right now in this present moment. Happiness is not acquired when you get that new job, new home or new partner. Happiness is available to you right now. Daydreaming about your future and deciding that things will be better once 'this happens' steals your present moment of joy and gratitude. There are many things in your life that you can be happy for right here, right now. Look around what do you see?

There were times when you wished to be where you are now, living life like you are now. Dismissing the present and what you once yearned for lacks gratitude and appreciation. Find joy in what is present in your life now. Detach from longing for something better. If you're not grateful for what you have, how do expect to have more?

Affirm

Happiness is available to me in each moment.

23 January

Your ascension journey involves you reclaiming your divine feminine/masculine power. Deep-rooted beliefs and wounds are surfacing for healing in your journey to wholeness. Your beliefs and perceptions surrounding situations and circumstances appearing now have deeper meanings and entail even deeper wounds. The depth of the wound or the belief can be measured by the magnitude of your emotional attachment and responses. Utilise these emotional indicators to identify what requires healing and love.

Your individual life and circumstances form part of the planet's collective restoration to wholeness. The planet reclaims balance through you, and with you. The divine counterparts masculine and feminine are seeking restoration and unification personally and universally. Your experiences are guiding you to reclaiming your divinity. Claim it.

Affirm

I claim restoration and wholeness for both my masculine and feminine aspects on my healing journey.

24 January

Feeling calm and balanced correlates to how much you're in the flow of life. Are you in an airy calm or emotional chaos? Resistance to changes creates dramatic emotions as you conflict with every circumstance. Activating the ego into protection mode causing reactionary defensive behaviours, rooted in emotional attachments.

When you trust the universe and what is unfolding, circumstances and experiences are catalysts for your growth. Submit to exploring all prospects with an open heart and mind. Free yourself of prejudices, bias, denial and emotional attachments, restoring calm and flowing energy into your world.

Affirm

I embrace change on my path to enlightenment.

25 January

Healing, releasing and levelling up are constant cycles on the journey. Increased consciousness enables you to see into yourself more deeply. Imbalances are identified quite naturally and your awareness dissolves and releases the issue quite effectively. More than half of the healing process is awareness and belief related. If you struggle to believe that your healing process, modalities or efforts will work, your healing will also be a struggle to transcend and release. Doubting your ability to heal gives your adversities the energy to remain in your life.

Rerouting neuro pathways by changing your beliefs is some of the most powerful work you'll encounter on your path. The impact of changed beliefs creates new paradigms and shapes the new world. Personal healing has increased responsibility with additional benefits.

Affirm

I am committed to my personal healing journey.

26 January

Divine timing is active as nothing happens before it's time. There is a connectedness that weaves everything together in the web of life. The divine holds complete awareness of how and when each particle of existence becomes interwoven, divinely weaving everything together with the collective fabric of humanity's consciousness. A plan this grand and complexed can only be orchestrated by divine energies.

These energies work through you and with you in each moment. Surrender to your higher heart and submit your will to your higher self. Stop forcing what's not flowing and let divine alchemy demonstrate how fate and destiny collide.

Affirm

I trust the divine to align me the highest experiences for my evolution.

27 January

Having faith in the unknown and yet unseen requires trusting the process of your evolvement, to lead you to where you need to be. Sometimes you're faced with circumstances and scenarios which seem extremely conflicting to your inner template of desires, wishes and intentions. This doesn't mean that they're no longer plausible either. Being logical trying to understand what is happening and fathoming your next steps is not giving you the security or confidence you need right now.

Overstand, that manifestation is not a linear process. How you get from A to B is not something that is known beforehand. It's something that is discovered along the way. Life is a mystery, let your individual process unfold and trust the universe to take you where you need to be.

Affirm

I surrender to the process of my own evolution.

28 January

Stop acting like a caterpillar when you're really a butterfly. Your cocoon status ended some weeks ago, yet you're acting all introverted and want to hibernate. The transformation has already happened, and the cocoon is gone. However, the physical you behaves as though it doesn't want to move into the new house and drive the new car.

It's time to feel what it is like to fly and see the colours of your wings. Your butterfly status is here to assist you in finding your new timelines in adventurous ways, exploring new territories with fresh perspectives in a light-hearted fashion. Recognise your beautiful new wings and fly into the new world fearlessly.

Affirm

I am willing to explore new timelines with my newly evolved self.

29 January

When was the last time you did something for the first time? You're engulfed with the energy of newness, are you using it? You'll never know what you're capable of if you never try something that you're scared of or that you believe is impossible. The human race has only advanced thus far because the past creators and inventors believed in their ideas and themselves.

All that you ever wanted to be and have already exists. You only have to align with it, which means taking the necessary action and, believing in yourself every step of the way. Limitless potential encoded in your DNA has been activated. You are the creators and innovators of the future. Only you can create your vision. The universe needs you to show up and show out.

Affirm

I am willing to express my creativity in new experiences.

30 January

You're striving for change yet do not realise how much has actually changed as a result of your evolvement. Your perceptions about life have completed expanded, you're moving differently, responding differently and thinking differently. Look at how you were several months ago. You probably couldn't have imagined yourself being who you are now, where you are now. You've outgrown many people, situations and circumstances as you vibrate higher. Your outlook on life has completely changed, almost automatically.

Huge transformations are taking place in your life, the shift is happening and changes are occurring as you're subtly morphing into higher versions of you. Recognise that you are the change you wish to see.

Affirm

I am the change I wish to see.

31 January

Pay attention to the ways in which spirit is communicating with you. Spirit uses many different ways to reach you. There is a unique language that spirit uses for each individual, dependent on their current energy/aura and consciousness. If ten people saw the exact same butterfly, in the same moment there would be a separate meaning for each individual.

Take time to study and learn spirit's unique language used to communicate with you. Keep a track of the signs in your journal to decipher your meanings and definitions. You'll find spirit's language in the synchronicities, animals, dreams, numbers, music, and intuitive insights amongst other things. Recognise the support that surrounds you daily.

Affirm

I am open to receiving all the signs the universe has for me.

1 February

What is happening, isn't personal it's universal. Just as the planet and the universe go through changes so, do you internally, mirroring universal energies. Personalising everything can create victim mentality and unnecessary attachment to passing energies. Start to view your circumstances through the perspective of the 3rd person. Like it's not happening to you. Only then will you be able to see that it's actually happening for you. Resistance may also be prevalent as you subconsciously wish things to stay the same.

Be observant and mindful of what is happening internally and externally. This is your power to overcoming the discomfort you may feel in this transitional period. Let go of the need to define your experiences and allow the magic to unfold without your influence.

Affirm

I am part of universal energies that work through me and with me.

2 February

Liberate your human self from the confined ideals you have created about spirituality. You have created so many parallels and your own pseudoscience that you're trapped in an illusionary world. This limits your ability to expand and creates harsh self-judgements about your life. Give yourself permission to be human without judgement. Only then, can you truly evolve.

Overstand that you partly chose the human experience to feel the plethora of human emotions and have physical experiences in the flesh. Feel the emotions that you believe are unspiritual to feel and have those experiences that don't make immediate sense. And then decide what is spiritual, and what is not. Liberate yourself.

Affirm

Spirituality only requires that I am authentically me in each moment.

3 February

Trust the new insights and awareness that are arriving. You may feel as though you had it all worked out and now new information is dismantling the very foundation upon which you have laid your plans. Dismissing options as being unattainable because of time, distance, finances and other excuses aren't reasons not to try one of the new options that you're presented with.

Trust the process this new awareness is not crashing or hindering your plans, rather redirecting you to what is more in alignment with your soul. This is not a time to be stubborn and dig your heels in and try to forge your original plans anyway. Accept the new awareness as a blessing that guides you to the highest path.

Affirm

I am open to flowing with and accepting new intel as it arrives.

4 February

Nothing in life is permanent; everything is constantly shifting and evolving. What was once comfortable and aligned can become uncomfortable as new alignments are achieved. In this process there are many people and experiences that form part of that evolution. Many people who were once part of the script have faded away. Experiences are rarely experienced in the same way twice.

Whether it was a joyful experience or a traumatic one, you're here now because of it. This is why it's very important to fully immerse yourself in the moment of now and experience the present. This moment can only be replayed from your memory bank. You can't have another identical experience again in real life. Savour the moments that form the days and years of your life, appreciating what you have, whilst you have it.

Affirm

I completely immerse myself in the experiences of now. Full joying each moment.

5 February

Who you were, is not who you are becoming. You have outgrown previous desires and dreams. The timelines that you previously aligned with have been recalibrated. Which is a direct reflection of the light influxes the planet has been receiving.

If you do not get what you wanted you're actually being redirected to something more in alignment with your current path. You've been advanced and fast tracked years past where you believe yourself to be. Feel the excitement of newness. Much magic awaits you.

Affirm

I embrace the new me and the newness that awaits.

6 February

Recognise your experiences and options as the stepping stones they are. Do not feel dismayed by the options you are currently presented with or by the route of your journey. They're not representations of your final destination. The path you walk is like an encoded map. Passing through certain terrains, crossing waters and reaching new territories, activates the opening of new terrains and territories to explore. These vast lands and waters have much wisdom for you to learn as you step through them.

Shift your perception to higher awareness. Know that all experiences in your life are stepping stones in your evolvement and enlightenment. Current situations and options are not the final destination. The best is yet to come.

Affirm

I am aware that each experience brings me closer to my destiny, on the path to enlightenment.

7 February

You're being introduced to deeper aspects of self. Encountering feelings, thoughts and insights that you never knew existed. Don't become resistant because you can't recognise these new unfamiliar aspects of self. In these new frequencies you won't find what you're familiar with or used to. What was in the old paradigm no longer exists in this new vibration.

The scripts have been changed, characters altered and scenery transformed. Assume your new role in these new frequencies. Prepare to be amazed as you open to experience more of your higher consciousness on the physical plane.

Affirm

I am open to receiving more of my divinity.

8 February

There are many truths which are relevant. Much of the theories and perceptions that you're downloading and tapping into, are real. There are multiple timelines running concurrently. Not just one or the other, as all are existing simultaneously. Whether it's political or spiritual, they all have relevance. None are right or wrong, all just is.

The convergence of these multiple timelines will culminate. The light and beliefs you hold now are influencing the direction of that culmination. Overstand your individual power to shape and determine the new world, staying present to consciously create new realities.

Affirm

I observe and acknowledge all of my downloads, only attaching to what I wish to manifest in the physical realm.

9 February

Recognise that your life is a continuous shift. Everything that got you to where you are now, were various steps on particular stones. Your journey has momentum and movement towards your evolution. There is not a circumstance in your life that you're incapable of handling. You're capable of utilising what is showing up at the moment for your benefit. Ditch feeling sorry for yourself and know that you're built for this and have been in training your entire life.

It's not what's happening. It's your thoughts and perceptions about it that causes conflicts. Your life will shift, and you will evolve regardless of whether you're accepting and embracing or resistant and defensive. Choose to surrender to the peace that's currently available to you.

Affirm

I surrender to the process of my evolvement.

10 February

Practise being present in this moment right here, right now. There is much time, energy and focus being spent on what is to come in the future. Likewise, with the nostalgic trips regressing into the past won't change what happened. Reflection is necessary however, you don't live there anymore. The future has yet to occur and will never match up to the moment of now.

Spending your energy rewinding and fast forwarding you lose the most potent moment of now. This moment is alive and full of life. Revel in it. Your momentary vibration is what creates your future. Being in alignment with your vortex momentarily will create more of the future you desire. This is about being happy, content and faithful in this moment of now.

Affirm

I am present in this moment full of gratitude,
contentment and love.

11 February

Apprehensive energy is what proceeds great change. It's natural to have anxieties about the future and fear of the unknown. What appeared as stagnation on the surface was in fact a deep revamping of certain aspects of your life. This also provided the space for you to heal and align with new templates.

As the cogs in the wheels start to take motion energies are released. What was previously hidden can now be revealed and realised. You discover why the pause was necessary and why certain projects, people and ideals aren't in alignment with you. Changes happen smoothly or dramatically. Either way change is imminent, embrace the unknown.

Affirm

I embrace the change occurring in my life.

12 February

The new creates much uncertainty, and you can become fearful to make any changes. You may be unsure of what is right for you, when in truth there isn't a choice that you could make that wouldn't benefit your evolution. Staying where you are isn't conducive to these higher frequencies. You will either be ushered gently into new timelines or you will end up there as external circumstances will conjure up that alignment for you.

It's time to embrace your soul's desires and potential. You can choose to walk there hand in hand with your higher self or you can resist the callings of your soul and create a turbulent journey. Either way you will arrive. Your soul has already agreed and is contracted to embody these higher frequencies, so you can channel your maximum light potential into your human journey and the planet. Answer the callings of your soul for they are leading the way to your ultimate destination.

Affirm

I choose to honour my soul's contract in this lifetime.

13 February

Time to focus on self-love and self-esteem, recognise that your world reflects how you feel about yourself. When looking in the mirror do you like what you see? Do you accept yourself as a physical vehicle for the divine? When you're aware of the energy you are, it is easier to respect and love yourself. Have an honest conversation with yourself and find out how you, really feel about you. Recognise the love that you are, how far you've come in your journey and know that you are a work in progress.

Any love you put out into the world multiplies and always comes back to you. Do not be fearful of sharing your love with others. Be at peace for you are beautiful and loved. Act with surety, confidence and the knowing that the universe loves you.

Affirm

I commit to loving myself more in each moment.

14 February

Love is unconditional and infinite, it is not bound to a specific day, time or place. For the most part you are that love, so do not let society determine when love can be celebrated. There is nothing auspicious about today, it is not connected to planetary alignments or cosmic energies. Mother Earth may vibrate higher today as everyone celebrates love but that is all.

Celebrate yourself and your loved ones today as you should do every day. Create your own love parallels and define what it means to you. When you'd like to celebrate the love vibe and where. Own your power of love and exercise your autonomy.

Affirm

Love flows through me and to me. Love is infinite and boundless, I am love.

15 February

Connect to your heart more. The constant struggle between your heart and mind is one that dominates your life. Your heart yearns for new people, places and experiences that your mind rationalises and deems unworthy or impossible, based on what subconscious data it can locate to keep a particular belief or programme operative in your world.

Learn to tune into your heart; it knows the truth. Start to follow where your heart leads, it knows where it is going. Your heart doesn't know rationale or limitation only the endless possibilities available. Connect with your heart to access the best navigation for all aspects of your journey and evolvement. Love lights the way.

Affirm

My heart is the navigation of my soul.

16 February

It's time to gain more awareness about love. The nature of unconditional love also includes every unconventionality of love that exists and that you are not aware of. Even though the essence of your being is unconditional love, you are still assimilating what that is, in your physical senses and reality. Your beliefs about what love is, obscures you from seeing and feeling the full abundance of love that is really available to you. Love has many disguises and doesn't always come packaged how you'd expect or delivered by your designated carrier on your preferred route arriving at your ETA.

Recognise the limitless ways love is available to you in every moment. Use your spiritual vision to see the love that is encapsulating you, and emanating from you. This is your love vibration, emitting your love frequency and attracting love to you in each moment.

Affirm

I am aware of the love that emanates through me and to me.

17 February

Nostalgia can be heart-warming at times however too much reminiscing can cause you to open closed doors and attach to what was. Once you've opened these doors again, you're also open to how you felt then, becoming overwhelmed you can start to believe that then is now. Letting go of the past emotionally and mentally ensures that you're not creating the same in your future. As a powerful creationist being aware of how you're attributing your energy, is a skill to master. Otherwise, everything else is creating through emotional default and subconscious energies.

You closed those doors because they no longer lead to where you're going. Reflection is natural especially pertaining to what you've learnt and how you've grown. Use your energy to purposefully and intentionally create the life you want. Remember that your energy creates worlds and enhances them. Spend it wisely.

Affirm

I am optimistic about my future and release my past with love.

18 February

Certain circumstances and situations can send your mind into overdrive. You've done a lot of work to master yourself. However, when the going gets tough and you feel as though your back's against the wall fear and feelings of disdain appear. Be aware that the higher you fly and the higher your consciousness is; the more different streams of information you can receive. In times of adversities or turbulence, you can have a sensory overload which can cause you to plummet to a low vibrational state, and create extra negative thought patterns and feelings. This is temporary as you master your new higher frequencies.

Try not to be self-judgemental in this process and remember the higher vibrations that you're now living in means you can also access the opposite lower frequencies too. Awareness will assist your navigation to mastery.

Affirm

I am aware of my senses and all they can perceive, always choosing the highest vibration available in that moment.

19 February

Honour your beliefs as what you know to be true for you will be challenged; dismissed and manipulated. What is being displayed on the world stage as truth and what the truth may be for others, is not the same as the truth that exists in your heart. It's challenging to balance these aspects through transits and intense corridors.

A huge part of your purpose is forging ahead with your truth regardless of the outer climate. Refrain from debating truths with others, this will just leave you feeling depleted and exhausted. Waking up every day and living your truth is how you shift paradigms, nobody else needs to live your truth or know of it, apart from you. After all, truth is self-evident and you are the evidence. Honour what you believe.

Affirm

I honour my truth in each moment, effortlessly.

20 February

Be reassured that all is well and everything is exactly as it should be. Sometimes when nothing is happening or when the opposite of what you want is occurring, restlessness, angst and anxieties arise. Rest assured that everything is happening for you, and not to you. Let go of attachments to outcomes and preferential routes to particular destinations. Be at ease with not knowing and allow yourself to be here now. Instead of projecting yourself into the future and being consistently concerned and worried with whats, hows, wheres and whens of your path.

Learn to relax into uncertainty like its best exhalation you've ever had. Let go, be in the moment of now and see how pleasant and joyful this moment really is. Leave the stresses of what's to come with the universe and fully immerse yourself in the experience of all the greatness that surrounds you and is available to you now.

Affirm

I am open to all that is available to me in this moment. I embrace all the goodness of this moment.

21 February

Remember to indulge yourself; it's easy to get caught up in the dynamics of just existing. Sometimes you're so busy making ends meet you forget about yourself. You've been very consumed with doing the work in so many areas of your life that you're forgetting the work, that has already been done. If you just keep on pushing forward all the time, without moments of self-recognition, the journey can become heavy like a burden, and your life dull.

You've accomplished much and need to revel in your own light. Make space to reward yourself every step of the way, self-validating who you are, providing you with confidence to propel you on your journey. Go treat yourself to that cupcake, massage, footwear, holiday or car you've been wanting. You've been working really, really hard and you completely deserve it.

Affirm

I deserve all of my karmic merits and acknowledge all of my efforts.

22 February

Embrace where you are in your journey, you'll never be too late or in the wrong place. You're exactly where you need to be, experiencing what is necessary for your evolution. Much time is spent comparing where you are in comparison to others causing self-judgements to arise. Your journey is personal and individual, overstand that no two people evolve at the same pace, at the same time. Embrace your individual steps on your unique path, for nobody else is going where you are or has been where you have.

Appreciate your uniqueness and own your part in collective consciousness. The puzzle wouldn't be complete without your unique energy contributing to the whole. Your originality is part of what contributes to the collective, be proud and own it regardless of what it looks like right now. Knowing the worthiness of your journey at this time.

Affirm

I accept my unique journey which leads to my unique destination.

23 February

Practise moving and transmuting energy from your body and bio-magnetic (auric) field. Energies can become stuck, stagnate and create blockages if you're not regularly engaging in activities or practices which involve all of the body. You may have experienced electricity issues, blowing bulbs, circuits and having static electricity issues. This can be reflective of the energies you're carrying and solar storms.

Incorporating energetic movement like dance, sports, yoga or tai chi into your routine, will assist in circulating and clearing any stuck energies and blockages. Increasing your positive ions and assisting in maintaining a high vibration. Master your energy through movement, your body and soul will be grateful.

Affirm

Moving my body transmutes dense energy and allows my energy to flow freely.

24 February

Start to know what healthy connections feel like and look like. You've had relations with many various connections over the years which have created behaviours and beliefs around communication and influenced your overall demeanour. The healthier connections can feel scary as there's little or no conscious effort required for it to flow.

As your perceptions have evolved so has your self-awareness and self-value. You're learning that authentic connections are naturally reciprocated, and there's nothing to prove. You really can be exactly who you are, no masks and be loved and appreciated. Healthy is unconditional, accepting and loving, erase all previous redundant data. Accept healthy when it shows up for you.

Affirm

I am open to receiving healthy relationships and authentic connections.

25 February

Limit your levels of suffering; you're suffering over your suffering. It is not your adversities that are the issue; it is your beliefs about it. You do not live in an unfair world! Please, erase this from your heart and mind. Everything that occurs on Planet Earth is divinely balanced with many universal laws. Operating from a sense of entitlement and unfairness creates righteous anger and will leave you trapped in your ego self.

If you continue to believe in unfairness you will perpetuate more of the same. You are not a victim, embrace your sadness, allow yourself to feel it and these feelings will naturally dissipate in time. Sadness and adversities are great teachers, which is a gift in itself. Be grateful for these blessons for they show you who you are.

Affirm

I accept my adversities as part of my soul's growth and evolution.

26 February

Your story and your journey are of great importance. You're a unique individual and as such have a unique story about your journey. You have overcome many challenges and adversities to be who you are now. This is the process of evolution. In order to expand and fulfil your potential, you'll need to transcend all the illusionary limitations that you've created, in order to feel safe.

Along your journey you've accumulated much wisdom from your experiences and your story will help others. Who have yet to experience, what you have, in the way you have. You have a responsibility to share your insights. Your journey is a gift, share it.

Affirm

My unique journey is a blessing that can assist others.

27 February

Forgiveness is a continuous daily process. Many situations, past events and people are being held hostage in your consciousness. The reason you're unable to forgive yourself and others is that you haven't yet completely accepted what has happened. Underlying resentment can create denial and victim mentality, causing a lack of acceptance. Overstand that everything happened for a reason and is all part of the divine plan. Your experiences have shaped you into whom you are today. Holding onto the negative elements of your story perpetuates your current reality with those same beliefs.

Liberate yourself, and others accepting your journey as part of who you are. Forgive yourself and others every time you remember. Healing and transcending whatever is currently blocking your path.

Affirm

I forgive myself and others in acceptance of all the experiences that have brought me here today.

28 February

Utilise your creationist abilities more effectively. Whatever you choose to focus your energies on naturally becomes more amplified in the physical realm. This occurs whether you're practising self-awareness momentarily or not. When your energies are focused purposely and intentionally you're more likely to manifest much quicker, more accurate physical versions of your ideals. Observe where and how you're attributing your energies. Are they aimlessly wandering waiting to see what direction the wind blows?

The ability to create and manifest has become supercharged and is your higher power to creating the new world. Only idolise, worship and take into your consciousness that which you wish to see magnified in your reality. Manifestation is now.

Affirm

I focus my energies on what I wish to create and manifest into my physical reality.

29 February

Give your mind a rest, as much over-analysis about your circumstances is creating unnecessary anxiety and fears. Your desire to know drives a constant internal inquisition, seeking facts and solutions for your current dilemmas. When you're unable to find the answers that you seek. The fear of the unknown arrives and makes you anxious about the future.

Release the grip on needing to know all the details, all of the time. Give yourself a break and go do something fun. The clarity will return if you allow yourself to come off the hamster wheel and refresh your perspectives. Mind your mind for it's the jewel of your soul.

Affirm

I allow all the solutions to flow to me in divine time.

1 March

Expect major shifts, miracles and magic. You have been wanting for the energy to shift in many areas of your life for some time now. Those shifts are starting to manifest in miraculous ways. Don't interrupt and resist change with the mind-set of 'this is too good to be true' likewise when desires may come disguised in chaos. You have wished, prayed and dreamed for your life to change. When movement starts occurring be prepared to move with it. Don't hesitate because it doesn't look like what you expected.

Everything is a stepping stone and needs to be utilised accordingly to reach your destination. Trust the process as you have learnt to trust the universe. Divine alchemy is at work in your life, embrace it.

Affirm

I embrace all the magic that surrounds me.

2 March

Release the extra weight in your life. You have released a lot mentally, emotionally, and spiritually. Does your physical environment reflect this? The journey becomes heavy and cumbersome when you try to take the past into your future. There are items that were once useful and fulfilling that no longer serve a purpose in your life. There are people that are not aligned with the new you, yet you're clinging to familiarity like glue. You want to expand yet you won't let go of what's weighing you down.

It's time for your physical world to reflect all the shedding that has been occurring. Holding onto people and items from your past that have no purpose in your future, will keep you stuck in the vibration you're trying to elevate from. Know when you've outgrown things that you no longer need and people that are not aligned with your journey. Only in this authenticity can the new you fully emerge and create your new world.

Affirm

I release all that is no longer aligned with my journey.

3 March

Independence is key to your journey. You've gained adequate wisdom which makes you particularly competent at navigating your own path. Your vision is unique as you are, others may never be able to see it from your perspective. You can't bring everyone where you're going. Let go of the need for others to overstand your journey and walk your path with you. Knowing who you are allows you to sense where you end and another begins. You have all the resources that you need to move forward. Self-reliance becomes one of your biggest tools as you evolve.

Create and maintain healthy boundaries. Your independence and wholeness will be reflected in others. These will be very stimulating, supportive and transformative relations for you. Maintain your independence whilst having fun with the beautiful reflections that surround you.

Affirm

I am independent in my journey, I accept my wholeness.

4 March

Anybody who is truly for you will never be against you. Are you surrounded by naysayers? Squashing your dreams, ambitions and beliefs? Sometimes those around you are unable to perceive your vision or ideals. They will deem them as impossible as their vision can't extend that far, and they don't want you to become all that you can be. These are not your people.

Those that are really for you, are already around you, or soon will be. Keep your fire burning brightly, for it lights the way to your dreams and ambitions. Nobody knows your world, like you do. It's time to leave naysayers behind and let your achievements do the talking. Be yourself unapologetically, you came to shine.

Affirm

My journey is for me to overstand.

5 March

Embrace all aspects of self. Your shadow is part of you and as such needs equal acceptance as much as all the other elements of you. Denial of the darker aspects of self prevents and blocks the blending of the complete you. Consistent recognition with only the lighter aspects of self negates the wisdom and knowledge the shadow has acquired. Your shadow self is what usually steps up and saves you if you're ever in danger.

Your wholeness beckons as all elements of you need to come together as integral parts of the whole. All of the intricate parts of you have adequate seating space at the round table, of which no part can be the head. All parts of you have relevance and will require inclusion to manifest your best life. Embrace and integrate your complete self.

Affirm

I embrace all aspects of self for my highest good.

6 March

Trust that everything is unfolding for your highest good. When being presented with situations and circumstances that don't quite make sense, or fit into your ideal projections, know that the universe is working its magic. Colluding with your higher-self designing a pathway to your highest good.

Trust in the unknown and allow the destination to naturally unfold. Attaching your energy to desired specific outcomes is blocking the multitude of opportunities and blessings trying to make their way into your life. Open to receive what is for your highest good.

Affirm

I embrace the universe working its magic in my life.

7 March

Be fully present on each step of your journey. Whilst you're rushing to your destinations there's little time to take in your surroundings and acknowledge what is around you. Similar to being on a super-fast train, only being able to see glimpses of the scenery as the train passes by. How much more would you see and feel if you were on a slower train?

Steady your pace, it's not a race. You will arrive at your destination regardless of how fast you're moving. What is for you will always be yours whether you arrive next week or next year. You'll never miss what is aligned to you. In that truth exhale, let go, and slow down. There is so much more fulfilment for you in this present moment, acknowledge it.

Affirm

I savour each step on my path.

8 March

Own your story with pride and conviction. We have all done things and been problematic at some point in our lives, to ourselves and others. Owning the less pleasant parts of your nature is part of learning self-acceptance and integrating your shadow with your light. When you accept yourself in totality others will too.

Practise forgiveness as often as necessary, with yourself first and then others. This will help you integrate and accept the darker side of your nature. Never dismiss or resist what made you who you are, and where you are today. Embrace all of the aspects that carved your well-defined character and gave you a unique lens in which to view the world. Your truth is relevant.

Affirm

I accept all the experiences that made me who I am today.

9 March

Realise that a change can happen in a moment. However, the preparation for that change may have taken many months or even years. What feels like repeating cycles and Groundhog Day is really the accumulating of more data. Your consciousness needs this data to evolve and create the necessary physical changes. Without this important information you're unable to gain the deep insight needed to evolve.

Hidden jewels are to be gained from these repetitive cycles. What was previously camouflaged is now in plain sight. Discover your hidden gems and make those necessary changes.

Affirm

I integrate all data in my consciousness needed for my evolvement.

10 March

You may feel a surge of buried stuff coming to the surface. Mostly being triggered by eternal events causing you to face some deep internal truths, that you never even knew existed. Making the subconscious conscious. You're being plummeted into the deeper layers of you, much of it rooted in traumatic experiences. You're being given an opportunity to look at things with a fresh perspective and an evolved point of view.

This internal reassessment of truths you've held subconsciously for most of your life provides an opportunity to change the foundation of what you believe. Whilst old truths are being exposed, the light of the new truth is revealed. When weaving in-between the two worlds know that both aspects have relevance. The new is seeking to establish autonomy and reign supreme. Let the healing continue.

Affirm

I acknowledge my new perspectives about my past experiences.

11 March

Unknown territory is beckoning to you. You've gained adequate wisdom and experience to trust yourself in new territories. Even though these new experiences incite fear, this is the energy that can change your life forever. Part of this soul's journey is about embracing and immersing yourself in the multitude of physical experiences available.

Life is for living and knowing when you can take risks, don't allow the fear to paralysis you.

Your choices are supported by universal energies. If you want the life you've been asking for it's time to step into the unknown.

Affirm

I step into new experiences with optimism, grace and confidence.

12 March

Flashbacks from past adversities are surfacing into your consciousness. There are past situations where you were not able to express yourself and how you felt. This may be because you were too young to do so, or as an adult when you were unable to find the right words or opportunity. Most of your feelings are rooted in not being heard or considered when you needed it the most. This can translate into your current circumstances with extreme frustrations when others are not able to comprehend you.

The overall theme is about learning the importance of your own needs and how to express them effectively. You've been ignoring your own needs for quite some time and you're changing that dynamic. Fulfilling your needs fulfils your soul and supports your evolution on the path to enlightenment. Ascension is all about you.

Affirm

I am expressing my needs effectively, I am heard,
my voice has value.

13 March

Become more aware of your value. Nobody is perfect and, everyone has their own shortcomings. Assessing yourself based on what you feel you've not accomplished has caused you to mark yourself down like a reduced item. Your value isn't measured by what you can achieve and who you can become. You've been worthy with tremendous value since you were born. Although your life may have been challenging and you've been through turbulent times, your value isn't determined by any of these factors, or by how anybody feels or thinks about you.

Worthiness is your birth right and your presence in this life's journey is enough to deem your worthiness. Don't look outside for external validation and confirmation of the love you are. Look in the mirror and see the truth of who you are, worthy from inception and beyond. The universe sees your value, its time you see it for yourself.

Affirm

I am aware of my value increasing as I gain
more self-awareness.

14 March

Trust and embrace the new perspectives that are being revealed to you at this time. Much has been hazy, unclear and uncertain. You are now being empowered with fresh insights into your existing circumstances. The signs and synchronicities are rapidly appearing at this time and the ability to decipher and interpret them correctly will create alignment.

The ancestors are ushering you to make choices and take chances in alignment with your intuitive insights. What you've been waiting for is now within your reach. You're being guided to your highest path. Read the signs the universe is showing you, its actualization time.

Affirm

I trust my intuitive insights arriving at this time.

15 March

Become more aware of your subconscious behaviours. There are some behaviours that are rooted in old belief systems that no longer serve you. Are you doing the same thing over and over again, yet expecting different results? Repetitive patterns in your life need to be analysed.

What seems to be the most familiar to you is solely based on a remembrance of an experience that you do not wish to repeat. Resonating and gravitating towards these patterns does not make the outcome any different. It only appears safe because of its familiarity to you. Practise awareness in the moment and choose a different route, only then can you arrive at a different destination.

Affirm

I release attachment to familiar experiences.

16 March

Become more trusting of your connection to source. You've developed a strong bond with source, your higher-self and spirit. The energy that you have been investing into your spiritual practices and disciplines has been noted.

Have faith in all of the higher powers that you're connected to and have been working with. Source knows exactly what you need and when. Trust in your journey, you're always on the path to having your prayers answered. Especially when you've been consciously connecting to the higher realms consistently.

Affirm

I trust my connection to source to provide what I need exactly when I need it.

17 March

You're developing great strengths along your journey. Tuning into spirit and adhering to your intuitive insights has given you much confidence. You've experienced how rewarding it is implementing your internal truths and those from spirit. Adequately demonstrating the power of self-belief, enabling you to flow more easily with life.

There is a multitude of various strengths currently available to you that you're able to connect to and channel in similar ways. Your template becomes more ingrained the stronger you become, magnetizing the magic to flow your way. Expect the potency of your life to change as you develop your connections with yourself and universal energies. Everything is about to get a lot deeper in a good way. Celebrate your strengths today.

Affirm

I am grateful for my strengths that I have accumulated along my journey.

18 March

Practise authenticity with yourself first, then others. Avoiding what your soul already knows and denying your inner truths creates circumstances and situations you'd rather not experience. Having high levels of awareness will allow you to recognise the transparency of what surrounds you, and how the holographic reality is instantaneously reflecting truth to you, in that moment. Hiding from yourself will only create experiences where things are hidden.

Dismissing the truth of your soul is no longer permitted on Planet Earth. Your vibration is demanding more and creating more. What soul truth do you need to acknowledge and honour today?

Affirm

I am authentic and transparent in each moment.

19 March

You may be feeling a sense of emptiness as a lot has been transcended internally and been removed externally. Much space has been freed up for the new to assimilate. You're now manifesting with the awareness that your thoughts, feelings and intentions create your reality. Becoming a masterful creator, even manifesting the things you don't want has provided you with valuable insights into how powerful the subconscious can be and how it can help you and not hinder you.

The new world and the new you are something to get excited about. Your physical reality is shifting into alignment with the truth of who you are and your authentic self is filling up the void. You're fully equipped to obtain your heart's desires. Claim it.

Affirm

I consciously create the life I want, manifesting the highest vibrations.

20 March

What's your narrative? What story are you telling yourself? Is it a new story? Or, an old story that keeps replaying? Some of your narratives can be extremely far-fetched, dramatic and fearful. Assuming the worst and expecting the same as before is how you keep creating the same experiences.

Dare to tell another narrative, one where there is joy, bliss, love and abundance. Replace the old story with a new one, literally. Don't allow your thoughts to run wild with any narrative that shows up. Consciously choose what the story is for you and keep that narrative. The most potent commodity you have in creating the new world is how you're focusing your heart and mind to achieve what you want.

Affirm

I create and believe narratives which align with my highest good.

21 March

Become more of a vibrational match for your desires. Many different circumstances and people enter your life as catalysts for growth and evolvement. These same circumstances and people are carefully crafted by your higher self, delivering the experiences that create the lessons your soul requested to learn.

Your attachment to these life blessons keeps this vibration alive in your auric field, attracting more of the same. Think, feel and visualise what you want instead of what's already happened. Detach from what has passed and align your vibration with your current desires. Be creative and think outside of the box.

Affirm

I align with my current desires, clearing looping attachments to previous timelines.

22 March

Become aware of the different seasons in your life. There are seasons for gestation, growing and blooming. All of your seeds have been planted, and you've been tending to your crops. There is nothing for you to do right now, apart from allowing your crops to grow while you take some much needed rest.

Whether it's a project, relationship or unresolved issues. It's time to retreat into hibernation to rest and allow the manifestations to occur. Any prodding or goading of these situations will not serve you at this time. Use this time for some much needed self-care whilst the universe works its magic in your life.

Affirm

I relax with confidence as my manifestations take physical form.

23 March

Without chaos and turbulence there would be no change or evolvement. As humans you are habitual beings and like being in your comfort zones with regular routines. When circumstances occur that disrupts your flow you can become very defensive and protective over the lifestyle you've become accustomed too. Some situations will demand that your life as you know it, come to a complete halt to incorporate what is happening. You then become flooded with angst, frustration and deprivation as your reality is threatened with change.

Blending your higher consciousness into your physical reality without judgements from either side is an alchemical skill to master. Accept change however it is showing up in your world. Apply your higher perspectives and trust that it's for the highest evolution of everyone concerned.

Affirm

I flow with the changes arriving into my world.

24 March

Let go of your need to be in control of everything. Trying to control how the wind blows is limiting how the wind is actually blowing. You don't always have to know the answers and be the 'knight in shining armour' for everyone. It's more productive at times, for you to step back and allow others to play their part too. The need to control stems from fears and beliefs in your subconscious about being controlled, preventing you from acknowledging and accepting the help that is currently available to you.

Let go of the fears that you'll have to do it all alone and the belief that there is no help for you. Surrender in the knowing that you're surrounded with all the assistance and love you need. Just step back and let it in.

Affirm

I have the assistance I need, I am never alone.

25 March

Trust your intuition. Deep down you know the truth, however, you're choosing to be consumed with your physical reality instead. You can continue to delude yourself or accept the truths that you already know. Self-acceptance of your inner truths allows your life to unfold effortlessly, whereas clinging to your present physical illusion only creates resistance.

Your soul chose to incarnate in this time of awakening and ascension to higher consciousness. Part of the evolvement process is gaining virtues so you can level up. Transparency is connected to the honesty virtue which requires you to be aligned with your intuition. You're creating your new world, make sure it's the one you really want.

Affirm

I trust my intuition and accept the truths I know.

26 March

Much is unravelling and your virtues are being tested. Do you believe the physical reality that you're presented with? Or do you believe in your deepest desires? One will diminish the other, dependant on where your belief is the greatest. The physical reality can take time to adjust to changes and will play out any subconscious doubts or fears. Stay centred and grounded into your reality and truth. Don't get distracted by the illusions that are appearing.

Acknowledge them without attachment, holding your inner vision as your most predominant perception. Exercise your humour as the illusions appear, noting previously unseen aspects. There's a reason for everything, maintain your frequency as the veil is lifted, untangling and revealing what is real.

Affirm

I believe in my deepest desires.

27 March

Overstand the power of your intentions. The clarity and nature of your intentions hold much power in creating the new world. Your individual intentions are part of the collective co-creation that blends together and creates magic. When the collective has similar individual intentions, new worlds are born. The purest intentions create the purest manifestations. Intend fully to own the life your heart desires in all aspects, with the quiet knowing this is becoming your reality.

The roots of your intentions are starting to bare its fruits. Recognise the power of your intentions by being precise and masterful in intending the life and the world you wish to be in.

Affirm

I harness the power of my intentions for my greatest good.

28 March

Practise honesty, truth is a frequency and where you'll find resonance. Your ability to feel the truth is enhanced the more you recognise, feel, accept and act upon it. As a bringer of light, you are unable to hide from your own truths.

You're already familiar with how the truth resonates and feels within you. However, you're choosing to deny and reject anything that's not aligned with your personal agenda, truth or not. Be honest with yourself and allow the truth to be revealed for what it really is and not what you want or need it to be. Acknowledging and honouring your truth aligns you with the magical flow of the universes, allowing you to receive what is truly yours.

Affirm

I align with the truth frequency accepting the truth.

29 March

Recognise the power of gratitude. Much liberation and empowerment can be found in practising gratitude. Reflecting back over your life, you're aware of what you didn't like and what created angst and adversities, as much as you're aware of all the heart-warming joyous experiences where gratitude usually flows naturally. However, gratitude for the less joyful experiences that were challenging and painful can be non-existent. When you disliked a particular experience part of you refused to accept it. This has prevented you from moving through it, transcending it and being able to access the gratitude for it.

Know that everything in your life has been divinely orchestrated for your evolution. Being grateful for all aspects of your journey will provide the liberation and empowerment to propel you forward. There is a reason why you are the way you are, embrace it.

Affirm

I accept all experiences that cultivated my path, I am grateful.

30 March

Question your loyalties and reassess your intentions. Are you loyal from a place of sovereignty? Or is your loyalty being influenced by external factors? You've been conditioned to accept and follow external narratives, committing your energy to things which do not serve you. Too much of your acquiescence is lost to people, purposes and situations that can't assist you in any way.

Reclaim your sovereignty and autonomy through only giving your energy to things which are in alignment with your personal truths. The new world is made to manifest through the highest authenticity each individual holds. Displaced external loyalties empower external agendas and not your own truths. The new world is reliant on your autonomy. Utilise your energy wisely.

Affirm

I claim my autonomy over my energy and attribute my energies to manifesting the new world I wish to create.

31 March

The fulfilment you've been seeking, is currently seeking you. You've been consistently focusing your energies on manifesting a more desirable lifestyle for quite some time. Your dedication is manifesting magical occurrences to create alignment in some form.

Remaining present, self-aware and conscious enables you to decipher which of your dreams are attainable from the different opportunities you're being presented with. If you want what you want, don't settle for anything less. Your refusal to compromise aligns you with what is truly yours. Choose to align with the realisations surrounding you.

Affirm

I accept the highest alignments for my journey.

1 April

Much lies beneath that which is overridden by your spirituality. Your connection to the spiritual realms and higher consciousness is not the ability to negate your humanness and physical vehicle. When you're constantly plugged into the higher realms, there are reasons and explanations for everything. This can easily become a subconscious coping strategy to ignoring how you feel.

Likewise, with your physical body it needs health and vitality to be physically strong to house the power of your soul and spirit. It needs just as much nurturing and consideration as your connection to source. You're learning to balance all aspects equally. Investing completely into your spirituality doesn't guarantee everything else will automatically be fine. Only equal investments can do that.

Affirm

I embrace all of the human experience and my physical presence on Earth at this time.

2 April

You may be feeling the need to be alone and withdraw to retreat from society. Alone time is the only way you'll process what is showing up for you. There are a lot of insights and emotions to be processed, and having the space to do so is absolutely necessary. You may be tempted to distract yourself from your inner feelings and thoughts to escape the intensity of what is building within.

Switch off and unplug from your usual schedule. Give yourself the time you need. You'll never be able to hide from yourself so create a space where you can just be and release what you're feeling, before your emotions overflow and pour out into external situations. Honouring your needs is always a priority.

Affirm

I create space for me to be with myself.

3 April

The right path is the one that you're currently travelling. Much energy is dissipated, concerned with whether or not you're on the right path. There are a multitude of different paths that lead to your destination, whichever one you're currently travelling is what is most suitable for your evolution.

Refrain from analysing the righteousness of your path and invest your energy into consciously being present in each moment, really fully enjoying the journey. Relax in the knowing that you're fulfilling your potential and soul's contract, even without your awareness or conscious effort. You're always on the right path, regardless of the trajectory.

Affirm

I am always on the right path with my soul guiding me each step of the way.

4 April

New energy awakens new clarity and new perspectives. What was once obscured can now be uncovered as veils are lifted, revealing illusions that have held you hostage. You may have been captured by your own beliefs, shadow or motives. Or external circumstances that dictate and limit your range of movements in the world.

A transformation is happening in the physical, aligning you with all of your spiritual, emotional and mental growth. What used to appease you can no longer please you as shifts in your physical reality are naturally occurring. The highest timelines become effortless choices as the truth shines brightly illuminating the way.

Affirm

I release all outgrown versions of myself with love.

5 April

Trust your intuition, sometimes what is logical may not be what is most beneficial for you. Logic and magic are not on the same frequency. Logic needs to make sense, whereas magic, is just magic. Do not be forced into making any decisions just because it may make logical sense. Check in with your body and your heart. How does it feel?

Signs are being delivered in various forms. Spirit is speaking to you, guiding you on your path, giving you signs every day. Be open to the route less travelled and the one which makes little or no sense. Trust yourself and you'll know exactly where to step next.

Affirm

I am open to receiving magic into my life in miraculous ways.

6 April

New beginnings come disguised as endings. In order for the new to take physical form something old needs to be released and removed, making room for what is to come. You've sat on the fence for long enough and know what is no longer serving you. Habitual familiar behaviours have you clinging to what you no longer need. Until you decide to let go, you are unable to expand into more of your potential.

Say goodbye; mourn the loss if you need to. Take some time to envision your life without the familiarity you've become accustomed to and let it go. The transition into the new is never plain sailing, for something new to be born, something old must die. Stop resisting the process of your own evolvement. Don't fear change, change fear.

Affirm

I release anything not in alignment with who I am becoming.

7 April

Connect more with the divine and expand your relationship. Do you feel as though you're coasting into the abyss with no real idea of where you're going or why? Do you feel unsupported and alone? You have access to unlimited support and guidance for your journey. Building relations with the divine will serve you greatly at this time. Whatever your issue is ask for help and it will be given.

Use daily prayers, meditation or just straight conversation to connect with the divine, that innate power within. Asking for help may not be easy for you, due to past conditioning and belief systems. However, the divine can't intervene unless you ask. Give your woes to the divine and watch the magic start unfolding.

Affirm

I ask the divine to assist me in my times of need.

8 April

As an adult you know that you're responsible and accountable for your choices, actions and words. You also know that there isn't anything you can't manage, or cope with, life has taught you as much. As a master of your destiny you're well equipped to deal with the consequences of your choices, and when necessary realign yourself with your true path.

When faced with several different options relax in the knowing that you have the insight, wisdom and confidence to choose what is right for you. Don't allow the amount of different options scare you into not making any choice at all. The path is mastered through trial and error. In order to know if something is for you, experience is your greatest teacher. Utilise your higher awareness and make a conscious choice about where you go from here. Your movements are supported, universally.

Affirm

I have the confidence to make the necessary choices for my evolution with confidence.

9 April

Experience the limitless energy that surrounds you. The universe wants to deliver to you. However, you're creating limits and blockages by expecting things to arrive in a particular way, in a particular moment. What if the universe has a different delivery process? And what if the delivery doesn't match your desired route?

Overstand that the details of your manifestation are of no concern to you. The various thought processes that you're spiralling into are constantly moving the goal posts. When you don't see what you want, the way you want it, doubt and fear start creeping in and you lose confidence and self-belief. Relax in the knowing that you are supported and loved. Focus on maintaining a high vibration momentarily and let your life unfold.

Affirm

I am open to receiving how and when the universe wishes to deliver to me.

10 April

Stay focused on your garden, no matter the weather. Magic is afoot as new timelines are established. Success, abundance and all that you desire is within your vast potential. However, you must continue to tend your garden. Believing that you can fulfil your potential is a huge part in physical manifestation. If your law of expectation is not aligned with your law of attraction, delivery will not arrive. Wanting the better career, house or lifestyle can't show up, until your belief is so strong that you expect it.

Continue to dream big remaining focused on your growth and expansion, ensuring that your thoughts and vibration are in alignment. You will reap what you've sown. Harvest time is near, and your self-belief is what determines the yield of your crop.

Affirm

I believe in the seeds that I have planted and continue to nurture them daily.

11 April

Recent shifts have caused you to wander in many different directions. Cosmic activity creating reflection and questioning of the past, DNA updates causing you to perceive things differently and light code updates ushering in new timelines. This all impacts upon your physical, ethereal, spiritual and light bodies. Your energy has become scattered as you integrate all these changes.

Call all of your energy back in to you by bringing your thoughts and emotions back from the nostalgic trips in the past and from projecting into the future. Affirming: I call all of my energy back into the now, whilst visualising receiving your fragmented energy back into your body. Repeat this for up to a week, two times a day, to recalibrate your energetic self into the now. Exercise being present and ground daily. Consciously tune into the now, completely receiving what is available for you in this very moment.

Affirm

I call all of my fragmented energy back into the now.

12 April

The fear you feel may have you stuck not knowing what to do. Becoming overwhelmed with the amount of options being revealed, you're feeling bombarded with new possibilities. This can lead you into feeling fearful to make any choices at all.

Ask yourself, do you trust yourself? When you have formed trusting relations with self, your inner dialogue is your best navigation tool for all life matters. Consulting with your inner oracle is where the truth can always be found. Use this truth to take an option. It doesn't have to make absolute sense now and you don't need to know all the details, it just needs to feel aligned with your inner intentions and desires. The rest will become clear once you have mustered the courage to take a new road. Your only failure is not trying. Overstand that fear is just an illusion. Don't be scared to live the life you asked for, it's waiting for you to align and release your fears.

Affirm

I trust my soul to guide me on my journey.

13 April

Honour your process, journey and those who came before you. What you're experiencing will one day become a legacy to those that remain after your departure. Just as your ancestors created legacies for you that have shaped the cultures of your families. There are many things that are possible now just because someone in your ancestral line has made it so. You have the same level of responsibility in this lifetime, creating ripples that alter the time space continuum.

Take some time out just to acknowledge all that is possible in your life and why it's possible. Reflecting on the efforts of those who came before. Acknowledge how far you've come and how much ground you've covered in your time here thus far. Realising and acknowledging that the challenges of being on the path come with huge merits that exist long after you do.

Affirm

I acknowledge and honour all those who paved the way for me to be here today.

14 April

Pay attention to your emotions, as they are your internal navigation system. Essentially there are only negative or positive feelings regardless of all the different words used to describe them. Whilst exploring places, people and relationships you may notice red flags, and choose to ignore them. Attached to perceived potential you forget and lose the truth of now. Don't become so invested in the potential of the situation or person that you compromise yourself now.

Being patient and loving doesn't mean that the square peg will fit into the round hole. These projects are tiresome and draining and will not lead you to your desired destination. Only delay and detour you, until you pay attention to your emotional compass and act accordingly. Open your heart and feel what is real.

Affirm

I acknowledge all that I perceive and act accordingly.

15 April

Let go of any excess physical and emotional baggage. Is your life filled with things that remind you of the past? Have you held on to mementos that remind you of past wounds? Rid your life of unnecessary items that serve no current purpose, other than a reminder of past experiences. Let go of what happened before. You already lived through it and retain memories in your consciousness about it. Having physical items as mementos keeps that energy alive in your life and clutters your physical manifestation process.

This clutter may also cause you to attract things into your life from that same vibration. Lighten your vibration and make space for the newness that's waiting to enter your world.

Affirm

I let go of all unnecessary items no longer needed.

16 April

Be open to new ideas, intimacy and love. What is truly for you can never be withheld from you. This is universal law. What is it that you cling to so tightly with a fear of losing? Be aware of possessiveness. You grip so tight that you may be squeezing the life out of your desires. This also makes you closed to alternative ideas which may also be beneficial for you at this time.

Loosen your grip, and open your heart. If someone is shutting you down or out, don't force any doors or minds to open. What is yours will flow freely to you. Trust the process.

Affirm

I surrender and let my life unfold divinely.

17 April

Create more balance in your life. Being obsessed with a particular area of your life is neglecting to other parts of your life. Your energy needs to be invested into all areas of your life, not just the areas where you want results right now. There may be discord occurring from important matters that have been 'put to one side'.

Learning to adapt to circumstances that you have no control over is a skill for you to master. Your adaptability will assist you in flowing through any changes in your life. If you want life to treat you fairly, you have to be fair to yourself first. Neglecting parts of self is what creates the disharmony. Restore the balance, invest your energy wisely and alignment is yours.

Affirm

I give my energy to all areas of my life equally.

April 18

You're way more capable than what you believe. You keep doubting yourself and the intel you receive. Your intuition is guiding you, yet you don't trust what it offers. You already have all the answers to navigate your journey.

Negating your gifts and the assistance they offer on your journey creates more challenging experiences for you. Ignoring your internal compass means you become more lost on your journey. Realign yourself with your divinity and demonstrate your acceptance with the relevant actions and changes. Your actions are the only confirmation and validation you'll need once you align with your capabilities.

Affirm

I trust my intuition and my gifts to guide me on my path.

19 April

Start owning and speaking your truth. Why are you so shy to speak your truth? Why are you afraid of owning who you really are? If you do not speak your truth how is everyone to know your boundaries, desires, needs and ultimately what makes you happy? There aren't many who are able to read your soul and see your authentic self. If you keep hiding and denying your inner truths, you will also convince yourself that they don't exist either.

It's time to claim your power and vibration on Planet Earth. No more time for shrinking to make others feel comfortable. You came here with a unique energy that needs to be shared. Open your mouth more and let the truth exist somewhere other than inside of your heart and mind. Then walk your talk, carving your most authentic path. Saying what you mean and asking for what you want creates the life you wish to lead.

Affirm

I speak my truth every time I talk.

20 April

You've been holding back on making some changes for a while. You already decided some time ago about your desired direction, yet your physical life remains unchanged. All the ground work is done, and it's time to walk your talk. There's no benefit to staying where you are any longer. The new world needs you to step out of the old and into the new timelines that you've worked hard to establish.

The preparation for a change may take many months or even years. Yet a change can happen in a moment; that moment is now. Be prepared to seize the moments that can alter your path forever.

Affirm

I embrace all opportunities to manifest my changes.

21 April

It's time to strategize and consider alternative paths. You're trying to move in a new world with old ways, getting you nowhere fast. Look into the aspects of the new world and the mechanics of it, deciphering what is the best way to navigating this new realm. Your old conditioning and beliefs have no place here. They don't fit in.

Resisting adapting to the new realms keeps you stuck in the belief that there are no changes. When you're the one that needs to change, to be able to perceive the new realms available to you. Bring your thoughts, words and actions in alignment with the new realms and leave the old ways in the old world.

Affirm

I am willing to change and leave my old beliefs and patterns in the past.

22 April

Seeking perfection internally and externally is hindering your progress. Being obsessive about perfection means that whatever is acquired or achieved in your world will never be quite enough, or good enough! You may even feel as though you're not enough and that you're under achieving and not fulfilling your own standards of perfection. Your perfection template that you've created has gridded your life with many expectations, which are mainly limiting for you. Perfection is to be faultless. Recognise that it's the faults which have brought blessons and expansion in your life. If you had acquired all of the elements, characteristics and qualities you desired there would be no work to do and no evolvement to experience.

Know that everything is as it should be. Perfect in its imperfections, including you! Let your life be experienced authentically in the moment without the need for perfection.

Affirm

I accept myself wholeheartedly as I am, I am enough.

23 April

Overstand the importance of rest. You will always need time of rest throughout your journey. It is beneficial for your mind, body and soul to take a break from your normal routine. In these rest periods you don't just physically rest. This is time for integrating all of the light code updates into your DNA and recalibration of your internal systems to accept these changes.

Disengaging from your normal life also has huge benefits for you, taking your focus away from your life, and your troubles. This will allow for things to surprisingly sort themselves out, while you take much needed rest and relaxation.

Affirm

I listen to the needs of my soul and rest when needed.

24 April

Slow down your pace. You're running down your path seeking your destination like you're trying to win a race. When there is no competition to see who can arrive first. Rushing around in this manner is causing you to try to force the flow. Moving this hastily makes you miss the importance of what needs to be achieved in this very moment. Being present and aware in this moment is the best way to navigate the path, enabling you to evaluate when and where your next beneficial step is.

Release the beliefs that you're not doing enough, there's no urgency. What's yours will always be yours. Your destination is for you, whenever you arrive. Keep trusting that your slow small steps will allow you to assimilate the best route with the most, undiscovered treasures.

Affirm

I am not in a rush to evolve into my potential.

25 April

Infinite possibilities surround you. You've diligently been tending to your garden and have been consistently creating, sculpting and revising for some time now. Being focused and committed completely unaware that your creations are being channelled from spirit. This kind of flow brings the magic of creating something out of nothing.

Going forward the possibilities are limitless. Being tapped into this type of magic you can accomplish all that you desire. Continue to allow the creativity to flow through you, and the opportunities, abundance, love and miracles will flow to you, magically manifesting what you need.

Affirm

I allow the creativity to flow through me,
manifesting the life I desire.

26 April

The new is beckoning. Arrival of brand new opportunities is an invitation to step out of your comfort zone and create anew. Not having any previous experience makes this an enchanting journey of discovery as your curiosity guides you through. Fearlessly embrace the new in a childlike manner, full of excitement and joy.

As the new world ushers you in surrender to co-creating something brand new in unknown territory. Openness and vulnerability are key to the alchemic recipe for magical manifestations. Your new vibration is waiting to break through in many forms. Answer the call.

Affirm

I am willing to co-create authentically in the new world.

27 April

Are you feeling the intensity of the energy compelling you to take action and make movements with your life? You've been committed to your intentions and desires for some time now. Having done all the necessary research and preparation it's now time to act upon your findings and trust your intuitive insight about where you're going and why.

Whatever your dreams are, action is required on your part to initiate the process of physical manifestation. The work has been done in all the other realms, making the physical occurrence effortless. Move fearlessly towards your desired life. Initiating the required processes and revealing your magical manifestations, confirming how much work you've really done. Step into your new life, it's waiting for you to own it.

Affirm

I am willing to initiate the processes for my physical manifestations.

28 April

Choose love today, forgive yourself and others. What are you still harbouring from the past? What wounds still hurt? Do these residual energies affect you emotionally, physically or mentally?

Begin by forgiving yourself and then others. Shift your perception about your life experiences as being a necessary part of your growth and evolvement. Holding resentment towards these experiences and people involved keeps you trapped in that cycle. If you hadn't had those experiences neither would you have the wisdom and insight that you've gained from experiencing certain trauma. Know that you're loved and worthy of all the love in the world. The key is to love yourself first, through your own pain.

Affirm

I forgive myself and others accepting all of my experiences as part of my evolvement.

29 April

Become aware of the range of alternative perceptions available. There are many different perspectives that co-exist, with all of them baring a relevance to the subject, some personal and some universal. Everyone sees the world through their own lens, which is either sharpened or distorted dependent on the experiences, beliefs, values and morals of each individual. Those with similar lenses may be able to share the same perspectives, whilst those with very different lenses can have opposing perceptions, which are equally relevant.

You may have 'blind spots' with obscured vision and need to consider alternative perceptions and to assist others in providing them with their alternative perspectives. Try to find the relevance in all perspectives even if it may appear distorted for you, only then can you include or exclude. Making space to consider and accept the contrast in perceptions also creates space for yours to exist in the world. We are one.

Affirm

I acknowledge all varying perspectives.

30 April

Surrender to the unknown, your desires about new ideas, romance and general life have passed the inception and conception stages. You're now in the birthing process. Your higher self gathers data from all of your lives present and past. In order to create the best physical manifestation that would suit you and your journey. However you're clinging very tightly to your own ideals. Let go of the need to control outcomes.

You have no concept of how your needs will be met. The universe doesn't work in sync with your current projections and ideals. The universe works for your highest good and all those concerned. When you're fixated on one particular way of physical manifestation, you're limiting and controlling how things can actually manifest in your life. Open yourself to limitless possibilities that surround you. The new you has many new expressions waiting to be assimilated. Trust that everything is divinely orchestrated just for you and watch the magic unfold. The time is now.

Affirm

I am open to receiving the limitless experiences that surround me.

1 May

You have power over your life, yet you feel frustrated because you're either giving your autonomy away consciously or subconsciously. Every time you fulfil external expectations: you surrender your will to those obligations. Learn what is beneficial to you and your life versus fulfilling what is expected of you. Some of your behaviours are habitual and may take a while to recognise. Your frustrations come when you're unable to fulfil your own agenda and meet your own needs, not recognising that illusionary obligations create this dynamic.

It's time to reclaim your life, for you. There is nothing more important than you and what your soul came here to achieve on this journey. Giving away your energy and resources unconsciously depletes what could be better invested in self. Take a good look at how your life is structured, and how you use your time. Everything is not worthy and only some things are supportive of your trajectory. Align accordingly.

Affirm

I reclaim autonomy over my consciousness.

2 May

You're dancing between the old and the new. This serenade can be quite exhausting, debilitating and confusing. You're revisiting similar or new issues like you've had in the past. This is to solidify your beliefs and new perceptions and to insure all fears and doubts have been completely eradicated. Even though you feel as though you have transcended these issues the re-visitation will cause you to demonstrate your evolvement and show how empowered you are in your new beliefs and mind set.

This backwards and forwards shuffle will continue until your new beliefs and perceptions are completely established and you are in your new timeline. The key is not to become your old self when presented with familiar circumstances. Applying your new ways to your old paradigm is the only way to navigate this space. You're more powerful than you believe.

Affirm

I apply my higher consciousness to all aspects of my life.

3 May

Illusions have kept parts of you captive for quite some time now. The truth of you is slowly being revealed, and there may be aspects you may not like only, because it does not align with your perceived ideals about your world. The shattering of Illusions can feel like a whole new awakening process as you integrate and process what has been discovered. Embracing the truth of you can be exhilarating and liberating once you accept it. However, processing these truths can destabilise you temporarily.

Higher consciousness is here to stay and no longer can you live in an illusionary bubble. High frequencies will shatter anything that is not authentic or true. Clinging to the illusions will only make this a tedious challenging process for you. Let it go, that which you are not can't live in the new world. Time to level up Light Warrior.

Affirm

I am willing to release all illusions in my reality.

4 May

Every experience is an opportunity to align closer with your truest desires. You may feel disappointed and dismayed when that relationship, career move or relocation doesn't end up being what you had envisaged. These processes allow you to accurately define what you do not want. As this awareness increases what you do want becomes crystal clear and easily identified.

Sometimes you can only really know if something is for you by actually trying it. Just like a pair of glasses or shoes, you know they fit well and suit you because you've tried them on. You're trying on different lifestyle ideals and its ok when they don't pan out as you had expected. You're en route to your authentic desires and that's all that really matters.

Affirm

I am open to trying new experiences to decipher what I really want.

5 May

Adjustments are being made as you encompass and embody more of your truths. The universe is shifting timelines and setting new trajectories, in accordance with your physical embodiment of your truth setting the stage for what is to come. Every time you own more of your truth timelines are adjusted and updated, as you demonstrate the willingness to be authentic on your journey.

Universal energies are working with you, expanding when you're ready for it. Your reality is constantly shifting and aligning with more of your potential. What truths you embody now shapes what can happen afterwards. The breakthroughs you seek are hidden in the truths you're afraid to own.

Affirm

I embody my truths in each moment.

6 May

Your intuition may not seem logical at times and trying to rationalise it or make sense of it will only take you farther away from the insight you seek. Intuition does not operate from a linear process that you can track. It's the divine spark that exists within you. The one that gives you 'hunches', 'tingles' and those 'knowing feelings', amongst other things.

Your desire to capture the essence of your intuition traps you into the whys and hows and stops you from flowing with it. Your intuition is sharp like a razor, and you have the X-ray vision to see beneath the surface. All you need to do is read the signs and trust them.

Affirm

I acknowledge and accept the insights my intuition offers me.

7 May

Step into your power and own it. This is not the time to play small or dim your light to make others feel comfortable. You have a prominent original message to share that has been cultivated through your past lives and experiences to date. Your life is the example that others can learn from. Everyone's story is different yet equally pertinent and has much value to humanity's evolution. There is much to be added to your story as you explore life.

Are you withholding your unique message with the fear of being unheard? It's time to speak up and own your truth. Everyone is not going to agree with your truth and that's ok. Allow others the space for their truths and this will create the space for yours. Be fearless with accepting the truth, and speaking it. Your power is dependent on truth to expand.

Affirm

I own my truths and am open to sharing them with others.

8 May

Your expansion is eminent and new experiences await you. Even though you may feel lost and slightly bewildered right now, be assured that new pathways are opening for you. Have faith and trust your intuition, for spirit is working with you and through you, establishing new timelines.

You've done the work to build the necessary relations with spirit. Despite how you may be feeling know that your connection to spirit and universal energies is strong. The process of evolvement is rarely linear. Reflect on your personal process thus far to recognise the magic of your unique evolution, realising that everything is in divine order.

Affirm

I have faith in the universe and trust that my new timelines are being established.

9 May

Be awake and very aware of the different people that are crossing your path. You've done huge amounts of healing and shedding of layers. Your wholeness is being reflected in those that you may encounter. Your soul family and soul mates who vibe on the same frequency as you, are coming closer. Like a magnet you're pulling them to you, as they're pulled to you. Vibrational matches are occurring. Staying centred and woke will provide the awareness you need to fully recognise and engage with this energy around you.

Those that you encounter are here to support your evolvement and expansion; you've been longing for such connections. They'll cause you to reflect and introspect, bringing out the 'best version of you', changing your perception of yourself and why you're here, being the catalysts for change. Be open to receiving, you're safe, go mingle and have fun.

Affirm

I am open to receiving new vibrational alignments.

10 May

Engage in new experiences. As fearful as the unknown may seem to you right now taking part is necessary to create the space for new opportunities. Avoid playing out the potential in your mind and envisioning various scenarios. That's how you convince yourself that the experience is unworthy, projecting your fears and vulnerabilities into the potential opportunity.

The worthiness of any experience can only be found in the actual experience. Life is an adventure, embrace it. Many new treasures are waiting to be found. Know that you are safe. Learn to trust your process, and everything will be revealed.

Affirm

I am open to engaging in new experiences and people.

11 May

The nurturing powers of the universe are giving you a nudge in the right direction. New things are out there to be explored, step into your power and claim what is yours. There are no obstructions in your way, and you are completely supported by universal energies. Every step you take right now is leading you closer to your dreams.

Keep moving with courage and faith even though past emotions and traumas may occasionally reappear. Allow these residual energies to move through you. You're not alone, the help you need will show up at the right time. You're on the path, keep going.

Affirm

I am moving closer to my dreams with each experience.

12 May

What feels like a tight limiting space with a multitude of external responsibilities is the pressure that's applied to initiate change. Overstand the pressure that is applied to carbon when it changes form. That form extends as far as precious diamonds and this is reflective of the process that you're in, changing form, from carbon to crystalline with your own personal metamorphosis. The pressure and restraints you're encountering in the physical realm are relative to the deep structural conversion that is taking place internally.

You'll only be aware of all of your restraints if you're physically presented with them; a lot have been hypothetical until now. Don't cower when you're faced with physical restraints that make you feel hemmed in. Smile knowing you've received more intel and as an agent of change, you can only break limits that you're aware of.

Affirm

I am open to receiving the limitless experiences that surround me.

13 May

Honour and acknowledge divine feminine energies. The suppression of her over centuries has caused much hardship and induced very linear ways of being and evolving. The divine feminine is alchemical, magical, blissful and sacred, amongst other things. Her exquisite energies reside within you and surround you. Her energy is being reawakened as consciousness of Earth and her inhabitants rise. The return of the divine feminine has long been a predetermined factor of the ascension process. Her reawakening is personal to each ancestral line dependent on the suppression that occurred in that individual lineage.

Honour her as the sacred portal she is. The gateway to the physical realm, creating and giving human life for you and all those that came before you. Connect with her divine presence and invite the magic into your life.

Affirm

I honour and align with the divine feminine
energies that exist within me and around me.

14 May

You may be feeling frustrated as you travel your path and are confronted with more obstacles and challenges. Are you moving too fast? Have the obstacles appeared to slow you down? It's not that these things aren't for you, it may just not be the right time. Sometimes there are other paths that need to be explored before this one can be open to you.

Slow down your pace. Take time to analyse your surroundings and recognise why this particular path may not be the best option for you now. Scan your environment and see what else is currently available to you. Be prepared to take a detour where you'll find hidden treasures to support you on your journey.

Affirm

I am open to exploring as many paths as it takes to reach my destination.

15 May

Reclaim your power and autonomy. Much liberation awaits you from the density that you feel is keeping you stagnant. You have the power to breakthrough any obstacle or challenge that you're currently faced with. When reaching certain levels of maturity, recognise that there is nothing you can't handle. You've overcome insurmountable issues to date, just take a look at your past history. Bearing this in mind, there aren't any consequences to your actions that your mature adult self isn't capable of handling. Your self-mastery has proved it.

Reclaim your power by fearlessly stepping into the new experiences that surround you. Much harmony can be found in these new realms. Courageously own what your heart truly desires. Only you can claim what is yours.

Affirm

I step into new experiences fearlessly.

16 May

As an empathic soul, you're very sensitive to the energies of those around you. How many people are you devoted to rescuing? Spending your energy on these types of projects will leave you feeling depleted. You can't rescue anyone from their chosen path as people mostly learn through experience. You trying to rescue them is a delay from them having the natural experience that will create the feelings to initiate change in their lives.

You may also be using other people's issues to hide from your own. Convincing yourself that the most humanitarian thing you can do is to be selfless and serve others: you can't pour from an empty cup. The energy being spent on rescuing others is better invested in saving yourself. Defining where you end, and another begins, is part of being responsible for your energy. Don't respond every time someone calls 'wolf', you're not the wolf slayer. Investing your energy into self-care will assist you in discerning what and who is deserving of your time and energy. Trusting divine order is part of knowing everyone is walking their own path at their own pace. Invest your energy wisely.

Affirm

I can only rescue myself and give others the space to do the same.

17 May

Recognise when you may need assistance and to learn to ask for it. You may be conditioned not to ask for help and this is true for many. The most supportive help you will receive will come from the divine. Whatever you need assistance with, you only need to ask. You're surrounded by supportive energies angels, guides, ancestors and ascended masters. Specific assistance needs to be requested so there's an invitation from you for intervention. Spirit respects your freewill and can assist with specific needs upon your request.

Building and maintaining relations with these divine energies you're connected with is paramount to the expansion you seek. All you need to do is log in, check in and share your woes. You're supported and loved; ask and you shall receive.

Affirm

I ask the divine for the assistance I seek.

18 May

Become more committed to yourself. Have you recognised how easy it is to fulfil your responsibilities to others? Compared to the level of commitment you give to yourself? It's very easy to use your perceived responsibilities to distract you from the commitments you made to yourself. Fulfilling someone else's needs before your own is not justification to ignore your own agenda.

Observe yourself and recognise if you're rushing to fulfil expectations all day every day or are you moving in alignment with your heart's desires? Reaffirm your commitment with yourself by being aware of what is most important to you and your journey.

Affirm

I am committed to my path and my journey.

19 May

You're an amazing intuitive empath and have done much inner work. Gaining much wisdom through experience whilst navigating your own expansion and personal healing journey. You may be feeling called to assist humanity in their healing journey; working with the earth grids, expanding your knowledge in a particular healing modality or delving deeper into your own healing. Embrace whatever your personal healing calling may be.

The collective consciousness is enhanced by each individual's ability to channel more light to Planet Earth. Become more aware of your responsibility as a healer, in this lifetime. The shift to higher consciousness is happening because of you, and for you.

Affirm

I am aware of the light I channel and the potential I have to heal myself, the planet and others.

20 May

When was the last time you looked into a mirror, connected with your eyes, and spoke into your soul? There is much truth to be recognised in this connection. Your soul knows your truth and the reflection in the mirror can't lie. No illusion, lie or limitation can be held in the reflection of your soul.

Spend some time connecting with your soul through mirror work. Speak positive affirmations of truth and see how your senses respond. Does your physical body accept the truths being spoken? Or are they being rejected? Your physical self needs to align with the truth of your soul in order for it to manifest. You can't create what you do not believe to be true. Aligning with the truth of your soul is the most empowering way to create your reality effortlessly.

Affirm

Mirror work connects me with the truth of my soul.

21 May

Honour your divine spark and shine your light. Your ability to know and see the truth is advantageous and allows you to move in directions that would otherwise seem risky. Use your spark to light the paths you're contemplating walking. Nothing can be hidden from you, as long as you're honouring your truth and following your intuition.

Dimming the light of your truth serves no one, least of all you. What may seem awkward is actually your magical life unfolding. Take the risks and shine your beautiful light. The universe is supporting your movements as your light shows the way.

Affirm

I follow the illumination of my light that guides the way.

22 May

Take responsibility for your health, it's the only real wealth you possess. It is easy to get distracted by life and negate yourself in the process. When the schedule starts getting overloaded, the first thing to always be compromised is your self-care regime. Your physical body is the vehicle that currently carries your spirit, soul, ethereal bodies and consciousness.

Prioritising yourself is very important now as your body is going from carbon to crystalline. Movement, minerals, water, nature's fresh foods and copious amounts of self-love are foundation to the process. If you don't take care of your physical body, the essence of you will reside in derelict unsupportive conditions. Taking care of your physical vehicle is a priority on your path.

Affirm

I am committed to honouring my vehicle and consistently nurturing me.

23 May

The moments that make up your life can be so captivating. Sometimes you can get so caught up in the momentum that you're not processing anything outside of your immediate physical life. Do your moments create momentums that lead closer to what you want, or further away? What you do in each moment creates the ripples that build your future.

Don't sacrifice your future for spending moments unconsciously with no authentic desire or direction. Life will give you what you want when you consciously choose that in every moment. Making that choice means you must know with complete awareness exactly what that is.

Affirm

I am conscious of how I spend the moments of my life that are leading to exactly where I desire.

24 May

Become more aware of your worth and the value that you have. Are you giving more than you receive? Are your relations balanced and mutually beneficial? Don't wait until the well runs dry, and you've given all that you have, to acknowledge that you've given too much of yourself. Lack of self-awareness can subconsciously encourage you to over give as your worth seeks validation and recognition.

Bring yourself into alignment with the truth of who you are. Connect in balanced ways and know that you are always worthy. The universe recognises the value you add to Planet Earth and so should you.

Affirm

I connect in balanced healthy reciprocal relations.

25 May

Be open to the limitless possibilities that are available to you. What you desire sometimes is not the best option that's currently available to you. The strength of your desires can cause you to become blinded to other opportunities that may be more beneficial for you. Beliefs surrounding self-worth can limit what you deem to be appropriate for yourself.

Take the blinkers off and recognise what you may desire is far less than what you really deserve. Other paths open to you, the question is, are you open to them?

Affirm

I am open to all the limitless possibilities that I am unaware of.

26 May

You're a sovereign being with your own journey to travel. There are too many opinions influencing your reign over your life. Personalising and believing opinions that are projected onto you gives them life and energies that do not belong to you. Once you believe these outside influences your reality becomes altered through them. How far you allow these opinions to seep into your consciousness further determines the authenticity of your reality. Does your world reflect your truth, or the opinions that are projected onto you?

You've done an immense amount of healing to clear your vibration from toxic energies. Don't allow yourself to become contaminated again. Filter everything, and be discerning about what you succumb to, in each area of your life. Only you know what's best for you.

Affirm

I am a sovereign being living a life that reflects my truth.

27 May

Save something for yourself. Aspects of you and your journey are sacred and not for everyone's ears to hear, and eyes to see. Learning what to share and with who is a skill to master along the path. Offering up all of who you are to any and everybody leaves you open, exposed and empty. There's a fine line between vulnerability and sharing for validation or justification. If you've lived a life where nobody listened and you were never heard, this can cause you to overshare without boundaries.

Everyone's evolvement is at a different pace; some are faster than others and some are more turbulent than others. Not every aspect of that evolvement needs to be shared. Some aspects are just for you to hold in your heart and know in your soul. Embodying the virtues of humility, modesty and grace is an innate power that belongs to you. Claim it.

Affirm

I honour my journey as the sacred path it is.

28 May

Traditionally you inherit when someone has died and left the earth plane. You have been focused and diligently clearing ancestral lines and the karma you've encountered on your journey. There are also many positive aspects to your inheritance that you have no awareness of yet. Through the paths that your ancestors walked many positive things were obtained and achieved. You have access to all of those achievements and, it's encoded in your DNA.

You didn't just inherit the negative karma; you inherited the positive karma too. These karmic merits will be unlocking over time as your life unfolds. Remain mindful that your ancestral karma is an extremely advantageous aspect of who you are in this lifetime. Honour those who came before: it is through them all things are possible, including you.

Affirm

I receive all of the sacred codes in my DNA as
they are ready to be released.

29 May

Even though your physical reality may seem chaotic and unsettling at times, maintaining your inner beliefs are paramount to remaining grounded and instilling peace into your world. You're an alchemist and have the power to transmute negative ions into positive ones amongst other things. The new world needs you to know that your beliefs are true regardless of what your physical reality is currently projecting. The physical world is always the last to align with the higher dimensions. Your beliefs shape and configure your physical reality, which can take some time to catch up and align into your physical realm.

In the meantime, the most beneficial powerful ability you have is to maintain your vision, beliefs and truth. Your beliefs are the foundation for creating your new world; create intentionally on purpose knowing what you believe to be true, in every moment.

Affirm

I believe in my vision regardless of what my current physical reality represents.

30 May

Practise observation and awareness, as ingrained behaviours may be causing you to unnecessarily challenge situations and people based on your old egoic beliefs. The new you has faith in your path and trusts the universe, whereas the old you had more faith invested into doubts and fears. As the new you assimilates your old beliefs try to grasp onto whatever they can to remain and retain recognition in your life.

Practising awareness momentarily will allow you to assess where and how this is showing up for you. Be mindful to respond from your heart instead of reacting from your mind. There's much introspection to be done as you separate who you were, from who you are. Serenity is found in aligning with your new authenticity.

Affirm

I am aware in the present moment with my new beliefs and perceptions.

31 May

Clear your environment externally and internally. You are holding onto and carrying too many unnecessary items in your life. Spend time regularly clearing your physical environment that you live in. Be authentic in your needs; if it doesn't serve a purpose, you don't need it. Likewise with your thoughts and emotions, are they serving your highest good?

Your conscious needs to be clear for your energy to move freely. Be honest with yourself and let go of everything that has no value to you. Clear, clear and then clear some more. Make the space for all the newness currently waiting to arrive into your life.

Affirm

I let go of all that I no longer need.

1 June

Happiness is not a destination. It's not a place you get to when you have more material worth, a better career or when you're in that ideal relationship. If this is how your happiness is cultivated, you'll create anxiety, frustration and perpetuate lack through never being content in the present moment.

Consciously choose to experience joy and fulfilment today. Joy is available to you right now no matter what your current circumstances are. Take a walk in nature. Look around, listen to the birds singing, feel the wind and sun on your skin, watch the children playing, stroke a dog/cat. Be in awe of life. Be grateful for all that your six senses are able to perceive on your journey. Happiness and bliss are yours if you choose to consciously align with that frequency for this is how true bliss is created. Allow yourself to experience happiness momentarily in every step on your path. Remember that happiness is always an inside job.

Affirm

I am aligned with all the happiness and joy available to me in this moment.

2 June

Your energy is contagious and affects those around you. Do you regularly dim your light to adjust to those around you? Fearing the power of your own light? Conditioning from past lives is affecting you, subconsciously, believing that there's some kind of punishment for shining your light unto the world. Some may not overstand your light, in awe of how you shine so brightly. Your light quota is equal to the amount of darkness transcended over many lifetimes. Be proud of the portal of light you've become.

Everyone is not going to accept your shine, for it illuminates their darkness; keep shining anyway. It's your shine that inspires theirs. Own your light regardless of what others may be doing. You came to shine your light unto the worlds, and you're influencing others daily.

Affirm

I came to shine brightly and proudly own the light that I have become.

3 June

Recognise how strong you really are. You're starting to actualise your strengths now, realising that it is your resilience that propels you forward. You've overcome many adversities and challenges to be who you are now. Your resilience gives you the confidence to know that you're able to face and deal with any circumstance that presents itself in your world. Your adversities provided the building blocks for your foundation upon which you stand so firmly.

Reflect on your journey thus far and accumulate just how many times you made it through that which seemed unbearable at the time. You've gathered so much spiritual, emotional and psychological strength along the way that you never even noticed how indestructible you really are.

Affirm

I am grateful for my strengths and the resilience
it creates.

4 June

Be conscious of your earthly imprint. Are your behaviours complementing the Earth or adding to her destruction? You're being called to be more responsible for the healing of the planet and self. What you do on a daily basis contributes to the collective. Are you aware of the impact of the resources you use like food, water, electricity and fuel?

Reflect on the impact your existence is having on Mother Earth. Adjust your behaviours where you can to contribute to her healing. She is forever giving, forever loving and forever sustaining you. It's time to give back and love her, like she's been loving you.

Affirm

I am in harmony with the laws of nature and align with the highest good for Mother Earth.

5 June

Check your intentions, are you giving based on what you can receive? Have you lost the joy of giving? The joy of sharing yourself with others freely? Admittedly spirit agrees that you have been taken for granted in the past, and not appreciated for what you bring to the table. However, this is not a reason to withhold your energy or act as though there is a scarcity of it. Neither is giving for the purposes of recognition or what you can receive in return.

Withholding your light and gifts is a disservice to your soul's journey. You came to shine and humanity needs you to show up authentically in your complete glory. Remember to give freely from your heart without expectation or agendas. These intentions naturally attract appreciation and recognition as a reflection of authentic intentions. Generously share all the love you are.

Affirm

I give with pure heartfelt intentions for the joy of giving.

6 June

Are you still sitting on the fence doubting yourself? Nothing in life is guaranteed, all you really have is this moment. You can sit on the fence as long as you like, pondering your situations and circumstances. However, that is not going to change your life. Not being able to predict how any particular circumstances or situation is going to work out is part of the journey of self-discovery and magic. Using your intuitive insights to navigate your path momentarily is how you carve the path to ascension.

You're not able to foresee everything on your journey. Somethings are magical surprises waiting to be discovered, which are only found on your journey, whilst walking whichever path you have chosen. You can't sit on the fence and surmise what may occur on any particular path. You need to get off the fence and go experience what you came here to do, then you'll know. Go live your life, stop hypothesizing about it.

Affirm

I am open to discovering all of the magic on my path.

7 June

There are limitless possibilities existing outside of your perceived potential. Have you been keeping your dreams as realistic as you can? Your perception of realistic is somewhat tainted by what you believe to be attainable. Dreams are where the impossible is possible, where there are no limits or restraints on what can happen. The realm of dreams is where you can be and have whatever you want.

Use your time in the dream realm to envisage the most magical life you can imagine. Leaving behind the constraints of the physical 3-dimensional world. Shrinking your dreams to fit into your perceived possible reality is limiting how much magic can arrive and when. Dream big with an open heart and mind, realising all that is currently available to you.

Affirm

I make the impossible possible with my belief
that it is possible.

8 June

Your soul has requested to learn many lessons in this lifetime, in accordance with previous life experiences and your evolution. Your higher self designs the details of the actual physical experiences that will give your soul its requested lessons. Data from all of your previous lives is scanned by your higher self, deriving a unique fitting experience that your soul will learn and evolve from in this lifetime, constantly devising new innovative ways in which you can learn. This is why the circumstances and situations that you are faced with are unfathomable to you.

The discomfort you're feeling are growing pains and growing pains can really hurt and are often worsened by resistance and attachment to your old self and experiences. Shift your perceptions about how you assimilate your experiences. Knowing that everything is in divine order and part of the divine plan, you can embrace each experience fearlessly and wholeheartedly.

Affirm

I perceive my experiences as part of my soul's evolution.

9 June

Assimilate your responsibility as a creationist. Realising that you're responsible on some level for what is being created in your world gives you the accountability for what is happening. Accepting that your physical life is you, not separate from you, and that you're not a victim of external circumstances. As difficult as this may be to acknowledge or accept especially in times of adversities. It's always easier to relinquish your responsibility and say that life isn't fair and find something or someone to be the cause of your discomfort. You would easily take responsibility for pleasurable outcomes and experiences, however, always finding a scapegoat for those not so pleasurable times.

Assuming total responsibility brings you into alignment with the manifestation frequency. Owning all of your creations and accepting your abilities as a co-creator is part of the ascension process and realising your power.

Affirm

I take responsibility and accountability for my manifestations, I am a powerful creationist.

10 June

Love cannot be expressed in words alone. Love is a verb so therefore can only be truly expressed through actions. Love is not what someone says, it's what someone does. That someone includes you. When was the last time you expressed your love to another? When did you last hug a friend? When did you last randomly call and check on someone you haven't heard from in while? When did you last tell someone how important they are to you and express your gratitude and affections?

Withholding the very thing you desire so deeply blocks you from receiving the same. If you want to feel love in your life, express and share the love you are with those around you. Love is infinite, and there will never be a shortage to give or receive. Free up the love and allow its infinite energies to embrace you.

Affirm

I am open to giving and receiving all of the love
that I am.

11 June

Overstand the abundance vibration, abundance is a frequency which you need to align with, in order to receive. It's not based upon how hard you work or how much you've given. Abundancy is your birth right, it's a vibration which you already have and need to attune to. Abundance is not solely financial and money related. Abundance comes in many forms. It may be that meal that someone else has made. It may be that smile from a stranger. It may be that unexpected help you receive. It may be your garden blooming vibrantly. It may be the love expressed by those around you.

Be open to receiving the plethora of ways abundance can enter into your life. Stop determining that you can only receive financially. Abundance is being rich in every area of your life and being rich has little to do with money.

Affirm

I am open to receive all forms of abundance into my life.

12 June

Time for you to focus on self-care, when was the last time you really indulged in nourishing your soul? Not just the few hours you may spend on a hobby, but the days and even weeks immersed in the calling of your soul's desires? How much dedication and commitment do you offer to making your soul content? Do you even know what your soul really desires? Do some introspection and investigate the true needs of your soul. Examine how you can accommodate this into your life permanently or at regular intervals.

Fulfilling the needs of the soul is often overlooked in the human experience, being too focused on survival and physical existence, neglecting the callings of the soul. Fulfilling yourself at a soul level changes your vibration and fulfils your physical realms effortlessly.

Affirm

I listen to and honour the callings of my soul,
nurturing them into existence.

13 June

Overstand the meaning of polarity in your life. The experience of unpleasant situations, emotions and circumstances are necessary for you to fully appreciate and recognise the opposite when it occurs. Disappointment and failure are experienced on the way to success and fulfilment. Likewise with love, many will experience what love is not before experiencing what love truly is. These contrasting experiences give you the full spectrum of human life, allowing you to decipher what is best for you and see what is truly available.

Polarity is universal law and exists with or without your awareness and acceptance. When you've been in unpleasant and unrewarding situations for some time polarity serves as the comfort and reassurance that better must come. You can't experience the negative without the positive.

Affirm

For every negative experience there is always also a positive one.

14 June

It's time to receive your karmic rewards. You've realised that true self-worth is more about who you are and living an authentic life than about what you own or what you look like. Adjusting your beliefs and recognising what true value really is has taken you through some painful blessons.

You've not yet embraced and acknowledged your complete worth. However, this is an on-going process for the most part. Even though value is not determined by material wealth, alignment with your true self-worth and values is often actualised in a physical reflection/manifestation. Abundance comes in many forms.

Affirm

I am ready to receive my karmic merits.

15 June

Question your love perceptions. Giving all your love and receiving none will leave you feeling depleted. Love is who you are, it doesn't require you to fight for it or win it, and most of all it shouldn't be exhausting. You can never be denied love, you can only deny the love you already are.

Choosing to invest your love energy instead of randomly spending it will create more of the love you desire. Love is the truth of who you really are, realise it!

Affirm

I accept and embrace all of the love I am in every moment.

16 June

You have levelled up in many areas of your life and attained many virtues. Most of the karmic past life restrictions have now dissipated and a more authentic you is able to emerge. However, do not become complacent, the universe will send you tests in the form of your old story.

You're being challenged. Are you whole? Have you really healed? Or are there elements still pulling you back into old wounds and conditioning? If you've healed you'll skip through any test that comes your way. Otherwise, you'll get pulled into the same perpetuating circumstances once again, showing that the lesson hasn't been learnt and there is still more work to be done. The universe invites you to dance a different dance, to do something different and create an authentic life, more in alignment with your new vibration.

Affirm

My evolution is demonstrated through my actions.

17 June

You're a powerful creationist sowing the seeds of your life with your thoughts. It only takes 17 seconds to create a physical manifestation. The energy created by your thoughts and beliefs is the message the universe receives and responds to, that shapes your reality momentarily. You will always reap what you've sowed and your garden will always be a reflection of your thoughts and beliefs.

Is your garden flourishing? Or is it overgrown and full of weeds? Only plant the seeds you want to see grow and remember it's only 17 seconds before the seed starts sprouting.

Affirm

I plant fruitful seeds with my thoughts and beliefs and my garden blooms with my creations.

18 June

Learn how to co-create with the universe. You have many desires that you would like to see manifest and it feels as though your requests are not being fulfilled. Take a moment to detach from your desire, breathe and let it go.

Your requests have been heard and registered, have more faith in your connection with the divine. Focus on what you need instead of demanding what you want. There are many ways in which your requests can be met. Be open to the magic that surrounds you. Don't limit yourself through your expectations. Remember you live in a boundless universe with infinite possibilities.

Affirm

The universe always provides what I need, when I need it.

19 June

Practise momentary self-awareness when situations arise that remind you of past wounds. Choose not to be limited by the truth that was created at that time, as the subconscious mind gathers data and builds very convincing stories for you. You have learnt to adapt to these stories as truths and this now causes you to behave in a particular way.

With awareness, your past wounds need not define who you are anymore. The truth is you have everything you need. Start acting like it! You are loved, you are worthy, you are a limitless powerful being with infinite potential.

Affirm

I free myself from my subconscious data that limits my beliefs.

20 June

Become more aware of your subconscious behaviours. Are you doing the same thing over and over again yet expecting different results? When you see the same red flags, why are you committed to investigating it all over again? You know what happens with red flags as you've been there many times before; it has nothing new for you, only more of the same.

It's time for you to draw upon your wisdom and navigate past the red flags, without stopping to have a look and checking if it's the same as all the others. You have the wisdom and awareness you need. Bringing it into your conscious mind is key to making it past the red flags.

Affirm

I have the wisdom and self-belief to navigate
past any red flags.

21 June

Alignment is occurring. You have doubted the possibility of the culmination of a deep desire for some time now that you'd lost all hope and even forgotten about it. That desire is still a dominant frequency within you, emitting vibrations subconsciously.

The universe knows what your desires are and also knows what is for the highest good for all. Your own personal long-forgotten desire has been woven into the universal plan. The universe hasn't forgotten you. Expect to receive what you believed to be unattainable and out of reach.

Affirm

I am grateful that my desires are on the way.

22 June

Treat your journey like the sacred path it is. On the path to self-mastery learning what needs to be shared with whom and why is crucial to the manifestation process. Human nature is one that will naturally seek approval and acceptance from others, and this can hinder your evolvement as you outgrow those around you. Trying to justify your movements with those who can't comprehend them only leads to scrutiny, planting seeds of doubt and fear that don't belong to you.

Self-assurance and self-reliance are necessary attributes required to overcome the need for external awareness and validation. Nobody needs to know the details unless they're part of them. Master the art of manifesting quietly, increasing how rapidly the physical alignment can occur.

Affirm

I manifest in silence and let my achievements speak for themselves.

23 June

Create more of a trusting relationship with your flow of life. Everybody makes mistake, this is a very necessary part of the journey, and a teacher that assists expansion. The concerns about potential 'mishaps' can leave you feeling fearful to move forward.

How will you know what's down the road, if you don't take the first steps? Let go of the over analysing, second guessing, and perceived obstacles. There is nothing to fear but fear itself. Go have fun, be open, trust and start making movements.

Affirm

I am flowing with life trusting my soul to guide me.

24 June

Realign yourself with your true values. There are beliefs, ideals, situations and people that are not reflective of your core values stagnating in your auric field and creating blockages. Remaining committed to any previous beliefs and ideals that you've already debunked, thwarts your growth. Likewise with circumstances and relationships that no longer align with who you've become. Loyalties can become cumbersome on the journey if they're not assisting with your destination.

Let go of the loyalty to what you've now outgrown and realign it with your current values instead. Aligning your values will benefit you and humanity greatly in creating the new world effectively.

Affirm

I am loyal and committed to my evolution.

25 June

Wherever you are on your path and whatever physical experience you're currently having, you are not alone. It's easy to get consumed by daily life and forget that you are connected to source energy and that the divine is always with you. Movements in the cosmos are activating aspects of your natal chart as the planets weave their differing combinations. The universe is supporting you through these transitions and values the beacon of light you're becoming as an integral part of the collective consciousness.

Trust in the knowing that in the eyes of the divine, you're perfect just the way you are. Wherever you are in your journey, you're valued, loved and appreciated.

Affirm

I am never alone; I am always supported by universal energies.

26 June

Let go of your worries and concerns. The more you stress over what you can't control or decipher the bigger it becomes. Being constantly focused on what is not present creates more of the same in the following moments, hours, days and weeks. Self-awareness will allow you to notice when you mind is becoming filled with anxious worries. Consciously realign your thoughts with something that you are grateful for in your life, and expand that vibration instead.

Share your woes with the universe, guides and angels asking for their help and guidance. They've been awaiting your invitation so they can assist you in surrendering all of your concerns, trusting that there are no longer any worries, and all is in working in your favour.

Affirm

I give all my concerns to the universe knowing
that all is resolved in the highest good.

27 June

If you're desperately seeking exit plans for your current situation, anything can seem appeasing. Every opportunity you're presented with is not necessarily for you. Some are reminders of what you don't want and reinforces what you do want. Some will test your virtues, integrity and principles. You'll never have to sacrifice your truth to align with anything that is truly for you. When you compromise yourself to accommodate opportunities you become out of alignment with your truth and your path.

Introspection is required to overstand if an opportunity is really aligned with your path and your journey. You may be hungry for change. However don't be tempted to just eat at every table you're invited to, as what you consume can drastically alter your trajectory.

Affirm

I stay in my truth as I allow opportunities to align
with my vibration.

28 June

Whenever things are removed from your life space is created for something new to arrive. Gains often come disguised as losses, wrapped in chaos and turbulence. This process creates expansions in various areas of your life. You may lose relationships and connections that were supporting illusionary beliefs about yourself. Creating space for newly aligned connections and experiences to be born. You may lose opportunities that weren't fulfilling your soul, encouraging you to try something new.

What is perceived as a loss is actually alignment with something better for your evolution. Grieve your loss if needed and don't cling onto what is being removed. Your anguish is rooted in fearing the unknown and doesn't really exist in your actual reality. Whatever is being removed and rearranged is for your greatest good. Trusting the universe enables you to trust the process.

Affirm

I am accepting of my losses on my path to enlightenment.

29 June

Acknowledge your power of freewill. You have the ability to choose over and over again. If something is not in alignment with your journey, you can always make another choice. Staying committed to choices which are no longer serving you blocks your growth and expansion. Remaining loyal to what was once a good idea will only leave you feeling powerless.

Assess where you're remaining loyal to desolate situations and people. Assert your free will and claim your power back, dismantling that which is not in alignment with your path. You're blessed with the ability to create your own reality, be grateful and choose wisely.

Affirm

I assert my free will to align with the life I desire.

30 June

Recognise the attachments that are creating stubborn behaviours. Why are you so determined that everything must go your way? You find yourself becoming angry and frustrated at life when things don't fulfil your ideals. You keep setting yourself up to be disappointed, not realising that you're the one setting the expectations. You're also the one who is angry, confused and demotivated when your expectations are not met. It's not that your expectations are too high, they're just too limiting. Realise that the world is not designed around your expectations. Loosen your grip on how things ought to be.

Overstand that until you recognise your responsibility in this perpetuating cycle, you will continue to manufacture negative emotional vibrations. Entertain the idea that your expectations do not include the plethora of limitless possibilities available, which are far grander than any personal expectations you may have. Trust the universe to conjure up exactly what is in alignment with your soul.

Affirm

I release my expectations, opening up to the limitless offerings available to me.

1 July

Motivation returns with refined clarity as your probable timelines become visible.

The fabric of your life has been pulled apart and dissected. You've discovered which fibres hold you together, and which fibres can cause you to fray. You're now able to weave a new, more resilient cloth and create a fabric with the most essential fibres available.

As the new world is being woven collectively and individually, those with the same patterns/fibres naturally align. An invisible thread is at work joining the similar fabrics together. Pay special attention to your intuition, opportunities and signs from the universe. Quality materials are available for weaving into your new world.

Affirm

I am open to receiving divine alignments with my tribe.

2 July

Overstand the power and magic of gratitude. When you have an attitude of gratitude manifestation is easier. Being grateful for all that you are, and all that you have will allow for magical manifestations to occur. You're in a powerful time to manifest your desires, and gratitude brings you into alignment with the abundance frequency. Allow the manifestation process to unfold naturally, without you pushing or prodding in anyway.

Your gratitude will be the magnet for miracles to occur. Overstand the truth, that there's enough for everyone, and that you are always enough.

Affirm

I am grateful for life and all that exists within it.

3 July

How aware are you of your power? If you never had your deck or divination tools, how would you be able to intuit what is happening? If you never had your crystals, how would you be able to draw on the qualities they offer? If you couldn't cast a spell how would you change the dynamics of your world? In the new world you're an innovator, finding new ways to do old things. You have encountered many tools and methods, some of which were created when we weren't living in higher consciousness, with access to our full range of abilities.

The tools and methods you've encountered are to practise with and learn about your abilities. Recognise that you are the conductor and the creationist. The skills and techniques you develop from various teachings are of your own making and empower your abilities further. Learn from old methods, so you can devise new ones.

Affirm

I shift paradigms when I embrace my creative spark and demonstrate accordingly.

4 July

Release the resentment you may be holding surrounding past wounds. The grief that you may be harbouring can cause you to be inconsiderate towards others, lacking empathy and compassion. New situations and people unrelated to your adversities that remind you of the past, can trigger any residual energies left from trauma. Reactivating past feelings and reinforcing the beliefs that were created at that time.

To truly transcend trauma and adversities consistent forgiveness of self and others is mandatory to your healing process. Do not be afraid to illuminate your own shadows with the power of your own light. Be brave and let it go, it's really not serving you anymore.

Affirm

I forgive all those associated with past traumas.
Every time I remember I forgive again.

5 July

You're starting to trust and have faith in unknown territories. Pushing past your comfort zones and familiarity, feeling more liberated as fear no longer limits what is achievable. All previous limiting criteria have been dismissed. As you move more into the unknown your courage becomes stronger with each step. Recognising that there is nothing to fear in the unknown is a huge achievement for navigating your path.

It takes a lot of courage to step out of your comfort zone, yet you've demonstrated that you're willing and able. It is your courage that makes the new feel exciting and exhilarating. Fear of the unknown is transcended as you're now comfortable in the uncomfortable. You never imagined that owning your truth could be so empowering.

Affirm

I take confident, bold steps on my path.

6 July

Become more open to receiving, you give a lot of yourself to others in many forms. How often are you allowing others to give to you? Why are you always saying that you're good, when you're not, really? Drop the facade of 'I can manage all by myself' and accept assistance when it's offered. Stop using 'I am good' as a defence to keep everyone out.

Opportunities are constantly arriving in various forms to align you with your destiny. Transparency is key to receiving the help you need. It's awesome to be of service to others, and it's as equally awesome to be served. Past experiences are not the template for your future. Trust and have faith in the new, the old really doesn't live here anymore.

Affirm

I am open to receiving from others.

7 July

You have an absolute awareness of what your truth is and perceptions about your reality. Many external confirmations are arriving in various forms, collaborating what you've known to be true for some time now.

These confirmations give you the confidence and self-belief to trust yourself and your intuitive instincts more. It's exhilarating to know that you already knew the truth. Believe in the truth of what you know now in this moment with increased confidence. Alignments of truths you've already known are appearing now.

Affirm

Truth alignments are appearing in my reality.

8 July

It's time to prioritise yourself: recognise that your responsibilities and commitments only exist because you do. Putting yourself first in everything is foundation to living a joyful fulfilled life. The more that you're rejuvenated and restored, the more fluidity your life will have. Pouring from an empty cup won't fill anything.

Listen to what your soul needs now and honour that. It doesn't matter if you break a commitment or don't fulfil expectations. What matters is that you're committed to yourself and how you feel. There's much to integrate and assimilate. Take as much time and space as you need to just do you.

Affirm

I prioritise and honour the needs of my soul.

9 July

You're currently challenged to release expired parts of your reality. You don't consume foods that are past their expiry date when they've started to decompose, getting mouldy and harbouring toxins. Continuing to consume expired energies lowers your vibration and makes you feel stagnant. Being aware that you're expending energies on expired factors only increases the impact.

Ask yourself, do you want what you had? Or do you want what is new? What expired elements are you still feeding in your world? Release the past that holds you captive mentally, emotionally and physically. The new needs space to exist and can't live somewhere that is already occupied.

Affirm

I release all expired energies with love.

10 July

Your commitment to your personal healing process is inspiring. Waking up every day and facing your pain and adversities takes a lot of discipline and resilience. You're gaining mastery in your personal healing as you've become aware of the continuous process it is, and not a one time, one solution for all. Learning to accept the things about yourself and your life that you'd rather ignore, deny and pretend never existed is courageous.

You're on the way to owning your complete authentic entirety. Look in the mirror with the light of your awareness shining the truth of who you really are, and see your journey of mastery in all its true excellence and transcendence.

Affirm

I am proud of my ability to heal, transcend and evolve.

11 July

Your life and the way you move in the world impacts many. You may feel that your random acts of kindness, words, gestures, smiles and general energy go unnoticed, when in fact you touch many souls daily. The energy that you represent is part of humanity's ascension process and contributes to the overall consciousness collective.

You're the physical conduit and conductor for the higher realms. Your aura is transmittable and transferable, spreading light wherever it goes. Never underestimate the power of your existence in this evolutionary time, illuminating shadows with your presence.

Affirm

I spread my love and light wherever I go.

12 July

Surprises await you that may not align with your internal plans. Some diversions and detours may occur to re-route your path. You may feel as though all of your plans are laid out nicely and the road ahead to be clear. Unforeseen circumstances may derail your intentions and may inconvenience you temporarily. In order for alignment to occur only the universe can conjure up relevant circumstances where fate and destiny can meet.

Expect the unexpected; this will enhance your ability to flow through changes. Accept whatever shows up with the knowing it is for your highest good. What you perceive to be your path is limited by what you believe you're capable of. The universe knows your full potential and will usher you into it. Trust the process.

Affirm

I flow with the unexpected and unknown,
knowing I am getting closer to alignments.

13 July

Be aware of self-sabotage; past experiences may be holding you hostage and dictating your life path. Adversities are your blessons where you can gain wisdom and evolve on your journey. Your remembrance of your past wounds gives them life in the moment of now and distorts your consciousness.

Today is the day to forgive yourself and others. Every time you remember, forgive again. What happened before isn't necessarily going to happen again, unless your fears are stronger than your desires. Ask the universe, angels and guides for healing and the guidance you need. Remember you are supported and loved.

Affirm

I release any past experiences that may
preventing my evolution.

14 July

You're accessing deeper levels of self. You've been committed to your healing journey and self-development for some time now. As you heal and transcend layers, hidden layers beneath are exposed and you're introduced to more aspects of your beliefs that have been holding you captive. Do not get frustrated with the process. What may seem like revisiting transcended issues is actually an opportunity to realise a deeper truth and gain higher perspectives to support your growth.

Stay committed to your development and embrace all of the hidden aspects of self that are entering into your awareness. This awareness is what initiates your healing processes. Don't resist going into places that you've been in before; there are still hidden gems that can be discovered.

Affirm

I accept all aspects of self as they are discovered.

15 July

Restore your life force energy. You may be feeling depleted due to over exertion and not getting enough rest and restoration. Whether its nutritional foods, sunlight, nature, rest or exercise now is the time to restore yourself and build your strength. This strength will be needed to manoeuvre yourself forward, becoming the physical conduit that will manifest what has been created in the other dimensions.

It's time to prepare and gather your stamina to fulfil your long-awaited desires. Various opportunities and synchronicities will show you the way. Just read the signs as they appear to direct you to your destiny.

Affirm

I nurture and restore myself regularly.

16 July

In this void in-between the old world and the new, feelings of nothingness encroach upon you. This liminal space is where you can envisage and create what you've believed to be impossible. Allow your imagination to roam freely without boundaries and limitations. What could you create if the impossible became possible?

Use this space wisely to focus on creating the new. The universe is requesting your participation in this co-creation; be brave and step into the unknown and impossible. Assume your role as a visionary creationist of the new world. The new grids are waiting to step into the limitless potential that surrounds you.

Affirm

I envisage the impossible becoming possible.

17 July

Honouring your truth is how you learn to navigate the path and life in general. Many factors will cause you to doubt yourself and the truth you know. Never feel obligated to justify your truth to anyone. Some will not be able to comprehend you and start to confirm your self-doubt, and that may include family members.

Staying true to yourself when your environment opposes your beliefs is the daily core work of light bearers. When you have faith in your truth, you're the only one that needs to believe it and know it. Continue to honour your truth in every moment. The new world is being created through what you believe.

Affirm

I honour my truth even if others can't see it.

18 July

Tune into your own vibration. You are met with many circumstances and people every day, how are they affecting your reality? How much stuff in your consciousness is actually yours? Are you holding and carrying other people's stuff, even in their absence? It's natural to hold space for others as you would like someone to hold space for you. However, once you've held that space for another, it is imperative that you don't take their stuff with you, into your life.

Learn to have compassion for others without emotionally placing yourself in someone else's circumstances permanently. Empathy also needs boundaries. Carrying the energetic weight of everyone's issues creates blockages and makes you lose clarity and it doesn't help in changing the issues for the person experiencing it. Know what you're carrying, and why, only then can you feel your own vibration.

Affirm

I release all energies that do not belong to me.

19 July

Overstand the power of choice you currently have. You may have become accustomed to things happening to you and responding accordingly. This pattern has caused you to relinquish your autonomy over your life, subconsciously believing through conditioning that you don't have any power.

Owning your power of choice and free will assists you greatly in creating the new world that you desire. Have a plan, ideal and vision and keep choosing until you get there. Make the changes before changes make you. You're a powerful creationist with a multitude of expressions that you came to share with the world.

Affirm

I continuously choose what is for my highest good.

20 July

When you have been diligently doing the work to better yourself and evolve, you will find yourself in experiences that test that evolvement. You're not going to repeat that experience unless there are still unresolved residual energies within you.

Whatever is occurring in your world right now is an opportunity to repeat what has happened before or apply your wisdom and choose differently. It's not Groundhog Day unless you want it to be. You are not being punished by the universe only pushed to evolve. Your expansion to higher frequencies and experiences are available to you, if you choose.

Affirm

I implement my wisdom in choosing what is best for me.

21 July

There are some old stories lingering around in your energetic field. You're able to see what lies beneath the surface and overstand the whys behind many things, providing you with insight and oversight enabling you to be more empathic towards certain situations and people. This awareness may have misguided you into believing that you should entertain certain stories long after that chapter has finished. It's your deep compassion, empathy, overstanding and loyalty to others that is continuously validating many never-ending stories.

There are new books that need to be written and you're re-reading random chapters from old books. These old books are being removed naturally and unexpectedly. Stay in your truth as your library of safety is rearranged.

Affirm

I release all narratives that no longer serve me.

22 July

Embrace your growing pains. The caterpillar always experiences some form of growing pains whilst emerging from the cocoon. However, the forms of catalysis experienced differ greatly, each time there is an emergence from a cocoon. Likewise, with your growth, many different aligned circumstances occur to shape your constant evolution. The process of growth is never a linear one.

Embrace any temporary discomfort as you make your way out of the cocoon knowing that there is beauty waiting to be revealed.

Affirm

I honour the constant process of my metamorphosis.

23 July

When you're presented with situations and circumstances that threaten your security, fear is the first emotion that surfaces. Fear magnifies the situation and adds extra momentum towards the result you're trying to avoid. When these situations arise holding your truth and your light is what creates positive outcomes.

As a warrior of the light, you have the power to change the energies and dynamics of circumstances and the outcomes, depending on what you believe and how you feel about the situation. This is how fear is dissolved. You are creating your own reality; become more aware and conscious of your ability to shape your world and experiment with it. More autonomy over your reality is available; claim it.

Affirm

I can alter my reality with my feelings, thoughts and beliefs about it.

24 July

Overstand the light that you channel. When you're a portal of light on a divine mission, in tune with the higher frequencies and are consistent with your spiritual practices, you will shine. Your light is on and so are your empathic abilities. People will see your light and be drawn to it. Like a radio transmitter you only choose what bandwidth/frequency you're broadcasting on. You don't decide who else is tuning into that frequency, making you visible to anyone who is seeking the frequencies you're transmitting.

Once you shine, you're no longer able to hide your light or keep it to yourself. Whether you're consciously choosing to share your light with the world or not, it touches souls every day.

Affirm

I am a portal of light, shining daily.

25 July

Release your fears as your life unfolds. You have many different options to take, and this can cause you to become restless and anxious in the process. There is no rush to make any decisions if you're really unsure. However, knowing what you want and not honouring that vibration greatly reduces your responsibility to consciously create the new world. You can either assert your free will and consciously choose the directions you'd like to take, or your direction will be chosen for you. The destination remains the same; it's only what route/experience you choose to get there.

This is a powerful time of manifestation and sitting on the fence is not serving your evolvement. Release your fears surrounding the unknown, be bold, take risks and step into the unknown, knowing all is well. Own your power to create your reality, your way.

Affirm

I consciously choose experiences that align with what I truly want.

26 July

Pay attention to your dreams. There is much activity happening in the dream realm, where you may be dreaming of people and places that you've yet to meet. Dreaming of past situations and people is an indication there is residual energies in your subconscious that may need clearing. Those that have transitioned are also using the dream realm to make contact with you. All of this astral travelling in the dream realm can leave you feeling exhausted like you've really experienced all that. The dream realm is as active as your daily life, and for some more active than their daily lives.

Your connection to the other dimensions has become stronger as you have become more aligned. That expansion includes vivid dreams, lucid dreams, premonition dreams, and visitation dreams. Become comfortable in experiencing and receiving additional intel from other realms. Go experiment and have fun whilst you sleep.

Affirm

I am embracing my dream realm experiences as they occur.

27 July

Anything not aligning with your highest good is being removed. Your vibration has increased, and anything not aligning with your new vibe is vibrating right out of your life. Your resistance to change creates discomfort as you've become attached to your comfort zone and familiarity, whereas the universe declares that it's time to live in the new world.

Just like when you graduate there's always a transitioning period before assuming your new reality. You're in a similar transitioning stage, now step outside of your comfort zone and realise what you've been asking for and what your new vibration is waiting to deliver.

Affirm

I align with my new vibration.

28 July

There is an intense purge of lower frequencies that have been harbouring in your energy field. This is a timely deliberate transcendence as a lot of repressed unknown traumas are cleared from your DNA/ancestral lines. There's a weepy theme with many tears being shed by many light bearers personally and for the collective. When passing through this corridor be mindful not to further repress, only feel and release.

The new timelines are being installed so expect physical manifestations of your deepest dreams and desires as they start to materialise in miraculous ways. This is a new trajectory completely different to the one you've been in so far this year. Embrace the energy that's coming into your world imminently.

Affirm

I release all that is no longer needed.

29 July

There is much to be surrendered; a lot of the feelings arising have echoes of limitations held in previous timelines. The story that you're telling yourself now, in reflection of your current physical circumstances has roots in previous incarnations. Feeling like you've failed at something because you never managed to complete it is an actual illusion. You weren't meant to and it's that simple.

Anything that is truly meant for you can't miss you. Let go of feelings of inadequacy, as those lessons have already been learnt. Your stepping into much more aligned higher timelines that you soul has not been able to encompass until now. Surrender all that isn't aligning in the time of now. The new is beckoning.

Affirm

I surrender any attachments to previous timelines aligning my energy in the now.

30 July

You're exactly where you need to be on your path, experiencing exactly what is necessary for your evolution. You're stepping into your new timelines or, you're already there. This looks and feels different for each individual. Some may be experiencing more challenging times than others, relative to where you are in your soul's journey.

You're not getting left out or left behind if you're not experiencing what everyone else is. Your journey and experiences have been uniquely crafted by your higher self to fulfil your individual soul's contract. Don't be tempted to compare your evolutionary process with that of another. You're the only one with your potential and the only one who can fulfil it. Honour your unique process.

Affirm

I am exactly where I need to be for my personal evolution process.

31 July

This is the in-between space where you're not where you were, or who you were and who you're becoming isn't fully yet established. The old hasn't completely dissolved, and the new is not yet formed. The in-between space can be filled with anxiety or excitement as you anticipate what is to come.

You're familiar with this in-between energy having experienced it before. However, this is unlike the others, this is also a collective in-between as much as it is an individual one. Collective ripples are being formed through individual choices. You're aligning with the new; get excited as all of your anticipations are about to be exceeded.

Affirm

I anticipate the future with excitement and joy.

1 August

Overstand that your wounds from the past aren't present. The circumstances and situations that you're faced with are completely new. Your research recalls subconscious data related to past wounds causing you to be trapped into the same behaviours and thoughts. This data creates unnecessary fear and insecurities preventing you from moving forward. Your life thus far has been structured around these subconscious beliefs.

The circumstances that created the pain which caused the wounds, no longer exist. Stop letting it define who you're becoming. Step fearlessly along your path knowing you're worthy and loved in a limitless universe.

Affirm

What happened is not what is happening, or going to happen.

2 August

You have tended and nurtured your seeds. The germination process is ending and sprouting is beginning. The commitment and dedication you have given to your journey is truly remarkable. You've shed many layers and your authentic self is now able to emerge. Alignment with your blueprint is inevitable now. Don't rush the process or try to manipulate how and when things are occurring.

Relax in the knowing that things are happening, with the confidence that it will happen. Go have fun, play and enjoy what is present now, whilst allowing the magical process to unfold and deliver dreams way more than what you could have imagined.

Affirm

I relax and allow my life to unfold effortlessly.

3 August

All possibilities are currently available to you in the field of co-creation. Make self-awareness a priority daily, bringing your thoughts and feelings into alignment with your heart's truest desires. The potency of current manifestation energies is instantaneously manifesting who you are. Be very vigilant in observing your own processes at this time. If you acknowledge any doubts, fears and beliefs confront them and release them as the illusions they are.

Be clear about what you want and have deemed impossible. Your vibration is your creation tool, setting the frequency for what possibilities can show up and how. Now is the time to let your potential roam, free and coincide with destiny; dare to believe in the multitude of possibilities.

Affirm

I align my thoughts and feelings with my heart's truest desires.

4 August

The pregnant pause is the space in-between the contractions, you may have noticed they have become more frequent encompassing every cell in your body. Each pause is an expansion that assimilates your increased vibration and heightened consciousness. Whereas each contraction can feel like you're taking two steps backwards.

You may not be able to see the whole picture or fathom the divine plan. Yet you're breathing through each contraction with trust, faith and tenacity no matter how intense the resistance. The divine is working through you and with you, guiding every step you take. You are the plan.

Affirm

I embrace the plan the divine has aligned for me.

5 August

Honouring your light and truth becomes more confrontational as you're being challenged to own your truth on much deeper levels that coincide with your feelings about loved ones. The task of speaking your truth has been overcome. Now you're faced with walking your talk and demonstrating that you are all that you say you are, and believe yourself to be.

There's an inner conflict of your feelings for those around you, versus the truth that resides within. This can be a constant battle as one always tries to override the other. Staying aligned with your truth becomes challenging as your morality calls for you to keep your truth intact whilst maintaining relationships with those you care about. Your integrity is your divinity in action, which is what acquires you the virtues you need to evolve on your path to ascension. Find the balance of strength, confidence and compassion to give your divinity space to live in your world.

Affirm

I harmonise with the truth of who I am whilst loving those I am connected to.

6 August

You're not as hemmed in by external factors as you may feel. Many of the restraints that you feel are actually rooted in your indecision about what you truly want. The unsurety about which direction to take is only because you have not yet decided what that is. Being presented with many options can be overwhelming, however there is an option that is most suitable for you right now.

Taking time out to assess your circumstances, needs and desires will provide you with the insight that you need. There will always be lingering doubts and fears surrounding any changes. However, your desire has to be greater than your fears to manifest the life you want. This provides the basis for harmonious experiences. Take the reins and decide what is currently best for you and what you truly want. Honour your decision consistently in all possible aspects of your life. Creating alignment with all that's already yours.

Affirm

When I know what I want, my intention is clear and so is my manifestation.

7 August

You may feel disorientation as timelines are merging and dissolving. You may feel like you don't even know who you are anymore, and at times you may feel as though your complete identity has been lost.

This is normal as the new is established both externally and internally. There's a period of nothingness and this may lead to you feeling confused and dismayed. There may also be subconscious attachments to conditioned behaviours, emotions and thoughts at this time in yourself and others. This will continue to surface until the new is completely established. Acknowledge them without attachment and allow them to pass through you, crying, shouting and screaming if needed. Let it all out, don't suppress anything that is coming up at this time. This will lessen as the new establishes more and more. Establishing new timelines and setting new paradigms is the nature of the spiritual warrior. Co-creating and navigating the new earth is not the easiest job. Your skills are admirable as you make light work of it.

Affirm

I acknowledge and release anything that no longer serves me, making space for the new to arrive.

8 August

Feel into the blissful energies available to you. Much of what you need to assist your evolution is available with a supercharged booster. You are sowing very potent powerful seeds at this time and access to your highest spiritual abilities are available for instantaneous download. Manifestation, creative downloads and informative dreams are just a few of the potent energies available to you. If you've been paralysed with self-doubt, unable to move forward, the confidence and courage to act in alignment with your desires is here.

Spend some time today tuning into cosmic energies. Feel the sun (Ra, the Sun God) on your face and remember that you are more than the physical body you inhabit. You are the soul and the spirit of infinity.

Affirm

I am basking in all the light codes and
frequencies available.

9 August

You're experiencing everything from a much deeper state of awareness. You may be feeling emotionally distraught as you're plunged into new depths of your emotional, mental and spiritual authenticity. Everything is enhanced with a microscopic lens, seeing and feeling the rawness of what's inside of you and outside of you. You've been doing the work to expand your consciousness and being in the higher frequencies enhances your sensitivities.

Utilise this deepening of your ESP (extrasensory perception) to realise your innate power. The ability to feel and see this deeply is a blessing with many beneficial factors for navigating your journey. Be grateful for the intensity currently rocking your world.

Affirm

I embrace my enhanced sensitivities with joy.

10 August

Use the wisdom that you've accumulated from your experiences to navigate your path. You may be faced with uncertainty and unfamiliar territory right now. However, this newness is a sign of your expansion and evolvement.

You're right to exercise caution as you proceed into these new territories, this will always keep you safe. However don't allow your caution to prevent you from making any moves at all. Like a game of chess, you have time to decide your move and these movements are continuous until the game has reached its conclusion. Likewise, your conclusion awaits if you're willing to make the necessary moves.

Affirm

I make moves that lead to my highest destination.

11 August

You've arrived into a new timeline where your physical expansion is starting to manifest. Feeling lost and more aligned at the same time can be bewildering. However, this is normal whilst you adjust to your new frequencies. A lot of your illusions have been dismantled and you're gaining fresh authentic perspectives. This maybe a turbulent process for you, resisting the new and clinging to the old can feel like being stuck in a continuous grieving process, let it go.

You're more aligned to your path then you've ever been in your journey thus far. Feeling unsure and perplexed, like the child who sees a Rubik's cube for the first time. Be patient as you familiarise yourself with this new territory. Embrace with awe, excitement and the inner knowing this is what you've been striving for.

Affirm

I embrace where I am in my journey with childlike joy.

12 August

You're embodying more aligned powerful aspects of self. Gigantic leaps in consciousness have occurred both personally and collectively. New pathways are opening up, and your choices are unlimited. Heightened sensitivities and empathic abilities make you feel everything so deeply, accurately and emotionally. Feeling disorientated is a theme until you completely assimilate the new.

As the physical reality is starting to reflect all of your work in the higher realms, you feel as though you're wandering around in a foreign country without a map. You're going through immense changes and recalibration. Be patient and compassionate with yourself as you realise just how much you've evolved.

Affirm

I nurture myself through my transition and recalibration.

13 August

Flow with your outer reality as it appears and unfolds. Being completely present in this moment is primary to enabling magic to occur. Whilst you're constantly focusing all your energy on the hows and whens, the present moment's opportunities are passing you by. Assume responsibility for your new higher consciousness, knowing that whatever happens is for your highest good.

The universe is ushering you towards your new timelines. Looking for ways for you to realise more of your potential and experience more of what the new world has to offer. When you're present, you can receive your presents.

Affirm

I am completely present in this moment.

14 August

Part of multi-dimensionality is the ability to have enhanced perspectives, for this realm and beyond. Aha moments of realisation are becoming more frequent now, as the alchemy of time and manifestation has completely changed. Try not to cling to your old perspectives as the new ones show up. Be grateful for your insights and hindsight allowing you to integrate and merge this awareness into your current timeline.

There's a sense of liberation when you surrender to the new and realise the limitations of your previous beliefs. See beyond the veil of illusions in your world and realise your authentic potential.

Affirm

I integrate all of my awareness for my highest good.

15 August

You're becoming a true alchemist. Integration of all the recent shifts has challenged you to the core, yet you've made it through and are evolving into more of your potential.

You've turned knowledge into wisdom, and your experiences will turn into magic. Staying loyal to your soul and your dreams takes dedication and discipline. Examine your experiences and acknowledge the gems that they contain, being thankful they were part of your journey. Alchemy aligns you with destiny, blessings await you, claim your karmic rewards.

Affirm

I am grateful for everything that made me who I am.

16 August

You've outgrown your previous limitations and what you thought you wanted has completely changed. Surrendering your previous narrative and letting go of what you had previously designed is more challenging than what you would've expected.

Switching timelines and quantum jumping between frequencies is exhausting work. Holding a vision for the future whilst letting go of the investments you've made in the past requires an internal knowing that what is to come is better than what has been. Break your attachments to your old mould and step into the new template that is more aligned with your divinity and authenticity.

Affirm

I surrender my past to make room for my future.

17 August

Stay grounded as old timelines are completely splitting away and being separated from the higher realities you now exist in. You may feel like lost parts of you are finally back and coming together as the old collapses. You're starting to feel a wholeness and fulfilment that previously eluded you, even though physically little has changed. Being aligned with the higher frequencies brings more balance as your spiritual self has more of a continuous presence in your daily life.

Establishing new timelines and setting new paradigms is the nature of the spiritual warrior and comes with much responsibility. As a co-creator and trail blazer it's you who gives life to what exists. Own it consciously, it belongs to you.

Affirm

I call all of my fragmented energy back to me.

18 August

There is an increase of light being consistently streamed to Planet Earth and her inhabitants. The light is so powerful now that anything hidden is being pushed to the surface personally and universally. Maybe you're experiencing intense surges of energy fuelled with intense emotions and thoughts which are relative to what is hidden deep within.

Become the observer, allowing these waves of light to move through without attaching to what is being revealed and uncovered. These intense light influxes will obliterate any hidden fragments of internal discord if you allow it. Healing can be painful, messy and traumatic: it can also be learning to trust, surrender and allowing the process to naturally unfold.

Affirm

I surrender to my healing process.

19 August

You can create anew in each moment. It doesn't matter who you were, what you wanted yesterday or what you once believed. You can choose and choose again, shedding as many skins as necessary for you to become the authentic you.

Whatever your conundrum is, whatever it is that's been holding you captive to a circumstance, situation or place is now ready to be released. Current energies offer you an enhanced opportunity to have clearer perspectives about where and how you can shed those skins you've now outgrown. Pay attention to your intuitive insights.

Affirm

I can recreate in an instant with my power of free will.

20 August

Be open to having new experiences. Realise that each experience you have is a stepping stone into your next experience. When life is perceived as interconnected continuous evolving experiences, your ability to move through changes, and make choices become enhanced. Being observant and mindful of what is happening internally and externally is your power to overcoming any discomfort you may be feeling in this transitional period.

However tempting it may be to live a life of familiarity, it's the new experiences that have the most to offer your expansion. Let go of the need to define your experiences and allow the magic to unfold as you play stepping stones.

Affirm

I welcome new experiences that assist my evolution.

21 August

Manifestation is quickening as collective consciousness rises on the planet. It only takes 17 seconds to manifest a thought. The longer you focus intention and feeling on the same topic the more amplified it becomes.

Envisage the impossible, limitless and futuristic visions now available to you. Expand beyond any beliefs you hold about reality. You're responsible for creating the new world momentarily. Create on purpose with your highest intentions and grandest visions. The new world belongs to you.

Affirm

I envisage my grandest dreams becoming my reality.

22 August

You're surrounded by aligned energies. Your intentions and your vibration, based on who you are in this moment attract aligned experiences, opportunities and people into your world. These are the co-creators for alignment with your intentions.

Magic is afoot, and synchronicities are aligning you with your path. Now is the time to actualise how powerful your intentions and feelings really are. Embrace the confirmations of alignment that are appearing in your world. Alignment is now.

Affirm

I embrace all alignments that I have manifested.

23 August

Become more aware of your creative powers as your ability to manifest your biggest dreams has increased as the frequency of the planet has sped up. Magnetizing your innermost feelings, desires, thoughts and dreams is a complete reality, occurring now. You know that you're a creator, now you'll physically be seeing your creations manifest more rapidly and consistently.

Let your divine spark flow freely wherever it dares to roam. You can create whatever you can imagine with your divine spark. Birth the greatness within that yearns to be expressed and life will reveal the beauty of co-creation.

Affirm

I am birthing my divine creativity in each moment.

24 August

Alignment is readily available to you. Many synchronicities are working in your favour to align you with the next phase of your evolvement. Your internal work is now being reflected in your external reality. Trust in the circumstances and people that are currently appearing in your world, they are the conduits for your growth and alignment.

Emit gratitude and stay attuned to that frequency as you start to assimilate how harmonious, blissful and joyful your life really is. Share the love.

Affirm

I am grateful for all the alignments I experience.

25 August

You're being introduced to a new vibe in the places and people you encounter. Don't feel fearful and become resistant because you can't recognise these new unfamiliar feelings. In these new frequencies don't expect to find what you're familiar with or used to. What was in the old paradigm no longer exists in this new vibration. The new people, places and experiences will astonish you, as you expect to be immersed into the same narratives as before.

When unfamiliarity appears in your world the new is making its presence known. Take the opportunity to explore what is being offered to you. You're writing a completely new story with new characters in a complete new movie. Choose characters and scenes that complement your vision, assuming your new role in these higher frequencies.

Affirm

I choose experiences that honour my evolvement.

26 August

Embrace where you are in your journey. The upgrades have been intense and quite rapid. You may be feeling disorientated and not quite know who you are anymore; feeling lost and experiencing a sense of loss, like something is missing. This can be relative to the aspects of you that have been transcended and left behind. Aligning with the new you and your new path will take some patience. In the meantime don't be tempted to return to you past behaviours as a way of occupying yourself temporarily.

Reflect and recognise your evolvement, what used to satisfy can no longer quench your thirst for life. The growth is real and your labour pains have been intense; you're finally about to see how the new you fits into the new world.

Affirm

I ground myself into the present moment knowing all that I've become.

27 August

Overstand the power of your intentions. Pure intentions have the power to cut through the most dense energies and environments, with a laser sharp precision. The purer your intentions the easier manifestations occur and, your desired outcomes reached. The purity of your intentions is determined by your love frequency and heartfelt desires. Being aware of the highest good of all, including yourself in any given moment aligns you with the purest intentions available.

Create deliberately on purpose and in alignment with your vision of the new world. Harness your power momentarily, wilfully directing your energies towards what you really want to create.

Affirm

I create with the purest aligned intentions.

28 August

It's time to do what's best for you. Mute the sound of external influences and tune into your needs and desires. You've spent a lot of your life living to the expectations of others and their requirements. When the majority of your life is experienced in this way very little energy is focused on fulfilling your own desires. Whilst you're busy fulfilling external expectations and pleasing those around you these external obligations become your priorities, and your truth starts to dissolve and lose value in your world.

In this time of potent manifestation, it is crucial that you're focused on your personal agenda and truth. It is great to be of service to others, however, remember to serve yourself first. Create the life you want, not the life that is imposed upon your kindness.

Affirm

I am focused on fulfilling my truth and my desires.

29 August

Much has sped up in your physical reality and things are moving at a much faster pace. You're exposed to more of your multi-dimensional self in these higher frequencies which causes you to sample several different perspectives moment to moment. What seemed plausible a moment ago can be dismissed in the next moment as you receive additional intel. You may feel unsure and unstable with so many different streams of information entering your consciousness. Going forward can feel like your slipping backwards as you're faced with more options that come with their own challenges.

Your multi-dimensional self is assisting you to reach fuller, higher perspectives about your personal life and collective energies, enabling you to make more informed choices about your overall direction. You're applying higher consciousness to your physical reality, co-creating ascension on your path to enlightenment. Trust the process.

Affirm

I am aware and utilise all of my multi-dimensional aspects.

30 August

There is a sense of renewal in the air, new energy, completely brand-new energy. Liberation from past emotions, beliefs and thoughts is a theme. The fog that covered your hindsight, insight and peripheral vision is being lifted. The projects that became stagnant can now be revitalised with a fresh sense of perspective. You can choose whether you wish to implement them or disregard them completely and start anew.

Whatever your choice the universe is supporting your trajectories. Alignments can be instantaneous in this energy, be conscious of what you're choosing in your career, relationships and personal life. You're emitting the vibrations that attract the frequencies you can align with. Invest your energy wisely.

Affirm

I align my vibration with the most beneficial frequencies for me.

31 August

Savour the emergence from your cocoon. The energies are feeling much lighter and centeredness is returning, restoring balance, clarity and ease. Just like the butterfly when emerging from the cocoon there's a whole new world to perceive and learn how to navigate. You're stepping into the new where old beliefs, limitations and rules don't apply. You're inhabiting new frequencies which have less restriction and more possibilities.

You'll align to more of your authenticity as you completely leave the cocoon and start to fly, assimilating the higher frequencies that you're now aligned with and open to. Take your time emerging and feeling out your new frequencies. Your avatar has awoken and wants to explore and have fun.

Affirm

I am exploring and embracing the higher frequencies available to me.

1 September

As children of light the colour of your auric field changes with your different moods. Your mood is influenced by your thoughts and feelings and sets the frequency for your overall vibration. When you're feeling positive this is the frequency that you're emitting and that is radiated out into the world. It's known as the holographic reality projecting your inner world and determining what frequencies can align with you and create the realities you experience.

In the new world, your feelings and thoughts are the currency that is exchanged to create the life you desire. Your frequency and vibration are more valuable than anything material in obtaining what you want. Aligning your thoughts and feelings with your desires is the alchemic recipe for manifestation.

Affirm

I utilise my energetic commodities wisely,
manifesting my desired life.

2 September

Allocate time to recognise and acquaint yourself with the new you that is emerging. You may not overstand why your desires have changed. You're automatically reaching for and wanting completely different things. You want to explore new places. Your food choices are expanding into new realms. You don't want to vibe with the same people and hang at the same places. You want less routine and more flexibility.

You've been doing the inner work diligently for some time now. The new you that is emerging is who has been uncovered and revealed through your healing process. Be patient with yourself as you get acquainted with this newer version of self and your new needs. Flow with what and where your heart leads for it holds your soul's truest desires. New world, new you, new dimensions. Go explore internally and externally. You're ready to embrace a complete new way of being.

Affirm

I honour the new me emerging and the newness
to be experienced.

3 September

Stay connected to your inner truths. Much is occurring in the physical realm causing you to question the validity of your truth and intuitive insights. The physical realm is a 3rd dimensional dense frequency, and is always the final stage of actualising what has already taken place in the higher realms.

The power of your truth and your belief in it is what constructs the timelines that create your reality. Remain focused and attach only to the timelines and realities that align with your inner truths, regardless of what the current physical climate may be dictating. It's time to own your part in consciously co-creating the new world with the power of your truth.

Affirm

I am aligned with my truths and have faith in what I believe to be true.

4 September

Your spark of divine creativity within you is ready to burst into flames. Whatever your endeavours are whether it be a new project, job, or relationship, your divine creativity is yearning to be expressed. Open yourself to the abundance of creativity that surrounds you, and life will reveal the beauty of co-creation.

You're attracting like a magnet now. Collaboration with others, who have the same vibration as you, will assist you in manifesting the finer things in life. Step forward with the knowing all is well and the universe is supporting your every move.

Affirm

I am open to receiving the abundance that surrounds me.

5 September

Your empathic sensitivities have been increased and you may be very emotionally sensitive. These heightened sensitivities can cause you to judge yourself and others harshly. Expanding into more of your empathic abilities will take some adjusting. Avoid heated discussions and emotional reactions.

You're able to feel more deeply into those around you and life in general. This is providing you with more intel to navigate your path. Amongst your overwhelming state of emotions, there is an amazing expansion taking place. Be extra kind to yourself and others. Practise empathy, patience and love. That is what you and the world needs right now.

Affirm

I am compassionate towards myself and others.

6 September

As the new is being grounded into your physical reality, hold an awareness of the limitless boundless space that you are entering. You've lived within limitations for so long that this new-found liberation can cause you to become fearful and anxious. Similar to horses who have their blinkers removed and can then see the fullness of what surrounds them. Do not allow the boundless possibilities to intimidate you in anyway.

This is what you have been working towards for many lifetimes. Your soul has been striving towards this heightened consciousness in a physical reality and now you're finally here. Celebrate; be joyful and grateful that you are actually experiencing a physical reality of such high vibration. This is the foundation for your path to enlightenment where you can become an ascended master. Acknowledge your achievements, you're demonstrating greatness.

Affirm

I embrace the limitless reality I am experiencing.

7 September

Your soul chose to reincarnate in this time of ascension to higher consciousness. On a soul level, you have always been aware of the responsibilities and challenges you'd encounter at this time. You have been preparing for this specific journey for many lifetimes, even though anchoring light to the planet and channelling it into your physical reality has been difficult for you to navigate.

In choosing to assist humanity's evolution process this was never to be a selfless journey. This level of consciousness encapsulates frequencies and realms you've not been able to access before now. When utilising this consciousness, you will recognise your ability to create, achieve and become whatever you desire. You're a masterful creator assimilating your capabilities. Your personal achievements become part of the collective's accomplishments. New paradigms are being created through you, being authentically you. Keep flowing.

Affirm

I am able to create and become whatever I choose. The new world is manifested through me.

8 September

As you evolve and learn more about yourself, the less you will be inclined to engage with circumstances and those who are not reflective of who you are and where you are in your journey. Some things will naturally fall away and disconnect from your new vibration, whereas some things will require you to actively disconnect. Staying in alignment with your current vibration is a skill to master.

The spiritual warrior knows that everything has its season and reason. You can't carry everything and everyone into the new with you. Accepting this can be challenging as you have formed attachments and bonds. Recognise what is not vibrating on your frequency and make the necessary adjustments. You may incur a period of grieving the loss of your old world and connections. However, liberation expansion and alignment to your new timelines are guaranteed.

Affirm

I align with all my new vibration has to offer releasing what is no longer needed with love.

9 September

Through all the healing you've been doing new timelines have been established. They arrive into your physical world through new opportunities, new people and random coincidences. Much work was involved in manifesting the grids for these new timelines with your creationist abilities. Some you may be aware of and some may have been cultivated through an awareness of what you don't want and may be very unfamiliar to you. Once you've chosen which timelines are most suitable, your job is to stay in alignment with your choices.

Practising conscious awareness of your needs and being the physical component that makes it all happen is a huge responsibility. Think less and feel more as thoughts can expand fears and doubts. Being authentic to yourself and others in every moment keeps you aligned with your true desires.

Affirm

I am the physical vehicle that manifests the higher realms.

10 September

Engage with your inner child and have some playful fun. Too much dense energy can make you feel dull and gloomy. Go be with the people who give you those deep belly laughs and sore cheeks from all of the chuckling. Make or do something creative like you did as a child; painting, dancing, tapestry, aeroplane models or matchstick building. Indulge your inner child s/he misses you. Especially when you get enthralled with the seriousness of life, do whatever it is that your inner child enjoys, expressing it physically.

You'll soon recognise the power of this playful expression and connection by the way it changes your vibration and soothes your soul.

Affirm

I am engaging my inner child in playful expression.

11 September

Your soul is consistently communicating with you to assist your evolution. Have you been paying attention to how you feel and your intuitive instincts? Your soul implicitly knows what you want and what is for your highest good. Your insights and feelings are not to be ignored or debated, only heeded. Overriding what you feel and intuitively know disconnects you from the source that assists your navigation.

You've integrated an expansion into higher consciousness. The only way for you to utilise this effectively is to pay close attention to your inner compass. Your heart and soul are guiding you towards what you need the most. You have the answers, you're just overlooking and bypassing your intel. What you want is already yours. Observe yourself and align accordingly.

Affirm

I am attuned to the vibration of my soul.

12 September

You're aligning more with the higher frequencies. Becoming a pro at surfing the waves, navigating the ebb and flow of density and extreme influxes of light. Enabling you to attract like a magnet as you allow yourself to be in the natural flow of life. Even though you may not realise it, your dreams are manifesting.

As much as you have been experiencing the heavy density of clearing, purging and releasing, an abundance of higher frequency energies are also simultaneously available to you. Expect random events, people and circumstances that will align you with your dreams. Stay open, woke and aware as you navigate the waves of ascension. Abundance is yours in many forms; receive it.

Affirm

I am manifesting my dreams when I encompass more light.

13 September

Much intel is being received through the dream realm. You're getting glimpses of possible timelines, some of which you have never consciously considered or even desired. These glimpses may be initially surprising or even shocking, as it extends far beyond the limitations you've created for yourself. In your vortex of creation, you have carved what you want, from knowing and experiencing what you don't want. The shape and form this can create aren't perceivable from your conscious awareness, until glimpses are revealed to you from the other realms.

Nothing is absolute or set in stone, your free will is the ability to choose what manifests into the physical realm. Open to the plethora of limitless possibilities. There's more abundance available than you're currently able to perceive. The new world is your oyster.

Affirm

I am getting glimpses of my potential realities
from other realms.

14 September

Your inner evolvement is being reflected in your outer physical reality. What you were once in alignment with and who you've been vibing with will significantly change as your internal expansion and upgrade integrates.

Pay attention when places, circumstances and people feel different to what they used to, your internal guidance system is alerting you to what is no longer resonating with your soul. Try your best to accept these changes without resistance and forcing yourself to continue with what you've now outgrown. All the necessary physical adjustments will not happen overnight, however, remain connected to the truth of what you're feeling to guide you to where you're going.

Affirm

I am aware of when energies are aligned and when they are not.

15 September

Align with the abundance frequency. You desire to receive much into your world, however you doubt and lack belief of your worthiness to receive what you truly want. This is how the law of attraction becomes conflicted with the law of expectation, as the universe always responds to the unique vibrations that you're emitting. Wanting something and expecting it are two completely different feelings that you're currently emitting.

The universe is waiting to deliver to you. Can you believe you're worthy to receive all of your heart's desires? Expectation is empowered when rooted in knowingness and beliefs. Know that you're worthy and expect to receive.

Affirm

I deserve what I am expecting to receive.

16 September

It's time to step into the higher frequencies that are available to you. You have observed and know what blessons you need to integrate in order to shed a layer, and shift to a higher consciousness. You are solely responsible for being the physical conduit for your higher self whilst on the earth plane. You frequently desire to become more and be more yet you're reluctant to assert your will in alignment with your desires.

Coasting along with life negates your creationist abilities to choose your reality consciously. Don't spend your life wishing and wanting more, when you're the physical component for those manifestations. What you want is wanting you, align yourself and be prepared to receive.

Affirm

I am asserting my will to align with my desires.

17 September

Release what is not in alignment. You're aware of what is no longer working for you and if utilised the awareness can propel you into finally letting go of what is not aligned with you. Ignoring your intuitive awareness and insight will only create more challenges for you later on. Overstand that your higher self is communicating with you to navigate you to the highest path on the shortest route.

Until you act upon your insights and remove what is no longer serving you, there's no space for newness to arrive. Utilise this time to finally close out what is no longer in alignment with you. Trust yourself, you do know what's best for you.

Affirm

I am listening to my internal guidance releasing all that is no longer aligned with me.

18 September

Overstand the dynamics of giving and receiving. Love is a verb and as such needs to be expressed in order for it to be actualized. Love, in every instance, is about the dance between you and a significant other, whether it be friend, animal, relative or spirit.

The dance is currently seeking you in many different areas of your life and requires your participation. There is so much waiting for you to receive, all you need to do is show up.

Affirm

I am showing up with love in my heart, willing to engage in the dance of life.

19 September

You already have everything that you need. Your experiences trigger a remembering of the deep wisdom your soul already knows. Your authentic self has been buried deep under layers of conditioning and beliefs, obscuring wisdom and truth from your senses.

You're now more aligned with your truest self and able to trust in yourself and the world like never before. Your intuition and instincts are guiding you to your highest path. Yes it is possible, you already came fully equipped to fulfil your purpose. Trust your process.

Affirm

I have everything I need to fulfil my purpose.

20 September

Recognise that manifestation occurs when your will is asserted in alignment with your desired destination. Expecting your manifestations to occur whilst you're moving in the opposite direction has only led you into disappointment. Part of choosing to be here in this lifetime is to be the physical component for your higher self. Doing what contradicts your highest good and desires, conflicts with your true purpose and creates unnecessary blockages and challenges.

Practise self-awareness momentarily to acknowledge where you may not be aligned with your highest truth. Assert your will and allow the highest energies to flow through you, manifesting your truest destiny and higher self.

Affirm

I am asserting my will in alignment with my higher self.

21 September

The fear of who you're becoming is creating resistance to the manifestation of the new you. The new template has been laid and much seems hazy. Your fear is a reflection of the doubt that your potential is even possible. Recognise that your trust and faith have transported you this far in your journey. The further you travel down your path, the more trust and faith you'll need, as the fuel that keeps you going.

The new you is awakening, surrender to what seems impossible. This is not the time to seek or expect support from others. This is a time of self-reliance and gaining independent autonomy over your life. The new you doesn't require validation or acceptance from anyone to exist. Know that the universe creates magic. Through your belief and trust in magical universal energies, you invite them into your world.

Affirm

I am aware of my infinite potential and surrender to the possibilities it offers.

22 September

Doing the opposite of what you truly desire sends contradictory messages to the universe, making you feel conflicted like the universe isn't working with you. What are you living which is not in alignment with your truth? You've outgrown some aspect of your life and something is no longer of any benefit to you whether that be a connection, a career, habitual behaviours or self-doubt?

Do some introspection and realise your true needs. You don't need to be over compensating for lack in any area of your life. Take an inventory to list what is helpful to your journey, realising what is hindering and unsupportive and choose to let it go. Don't allow your fear or doubt to make choices for you. Align your behaviours with your desires, now is the time to align with your authentic path.

Affirm

I am aligning with my truth, navigating to my authentic path.

23 September

New frequencies have opened for you to anchor into your consciousness. You may not be feeling this, as you may be overwhelmed with the amount of light flooding the planet and looping ingrained patterns from the past. Where you were previously confronted with brick walls they have since been demolished and the landscape is now vast, fertile and never-ending. This is the levels of newness available to you.

Anchoring these new frequencies will take time and an awareness of their existence as you can't utilise something you've no knowledge about. Let go of the physical world and take some time out to be still and feel the new energies that are now available to you; they hold the answers you seek. Align and anchor, harnessing the new energies available to you.

Affirm

I am still and acknowledging all the new
frequencies available to me.

24 September

Focus your energy on the new. You may be feeling empty and lost now the hazy cluster of denseness has dissipated. You'll feel lost and ungrounded as you find the new you and ground into your new timelines. You'll feel emptiness until you're filled up again. In this energetic lull it's easy to feel depressed, unmotivated and disconnected. Don't be tempted to re-attach to old patterns and behaviours to fill the gap. You're really in a new frequency and need to adjust to the newness available within you and around you. The physical you is aligning with all of these changes and feeling this void-type energy is part of that expansion.

Be consciously aware in the now and create intently and purposefully. Your energy has laser sharp precision and needs to be directed into creating anew. You've got a blank canvas and a complete reset; you can create whatever you want from zero point. Ensure it's new, different, original and aligned with the authentic you.

Affirm

I am filling myself up with all the newness available to me.

25 September

You may be feeling a sense of floatiness as you're not currently anchored to what was; the old timeline and new timelines are not yet formed. Everything can feel like a permanent hazy day. In this space is where you're creating the new; many old patterns and beliefs will surface to remain attached and relevant in your New World. The denser aspects of you are clinging on for their survival and they will be found in nearly every person and situation you meet.

Hold the awareness of what is real for you now in this moment. Eliminate the distortions with the power of your truth and light that shines from within. Illusionary past beliefs cannot be allowed to create your future. Diminish the old story every time the book opens.

Affirm

I release all narratives that are no longer relevant to my journey.

26 September

The energies may have you feeling slightly anxious, out of sync and wondering where you are now. This is all relative to grounding into new timelines. You may feel temporarily disconnected as you are no longer connected to the old and the new is not yet certain or established. The space can feel very unfamiliar, as you're not willing to go back to the security and comfort of the old and you feel something new is beckoning.

Take time to become comfortable in the uncomfortable and unknowing spaces. Take refuge in knowing that you don't have all of the answers, and that's okay. You know they're on the way as you have trust and faith in yourself, the universe and the energies that work with you, and through you. Uncertain spaces are beneficial to your evolution, assisting you to realign with the limitless potential that surrounds you. Embrace the unknown.

Affirm

I am comfortable in the uncomfortable,
enhancing my ability to flow through changes.

27 September

Practise silence and observation. Many words and conversations are spoken without any real purpose or intent, and sometimes that intent is based in ego, fear or anger. Many people are being flooded with their suppressed emotional traumas, and many of those people may not be consciously on the path or aware of their spiritual self. People may lash out for no apparent reason. Some may be highly strung and stressed out. Repressed emotions are seeking release and expression. This can also be true for those who are on the path and have subconscious traumas, including you.

If you find yourself getting into a strange interaction or an obscure conversation exchanging meaningless words, it's easy to be triggered and start responding from your own wounds. Avoid dissipating your energy by engaging with these distractions. Observe what is being communicated without absorbing it into your energetic field. Everything is not worthy of a response much less your reaction. Silence yourself and save your energy.

Affirm

I observe myself and others engaging in
purposeful interactions.

28 September

Become more aware of your growth. You've come through another ride on the ascension highway only in preparation to enter another. The ground beneath you keeps on moving and forming new pathways and possibilities. New grids are being formed momentarily and the old disintegrating. Much has felt like a whirlwind as the speed of the light code updates to your DNA have increased; assisting a rapid elevation in consciousness.

Reflect on where you were a few months ago and recognise how far you've come. Your expansion has always been imminent and your efficiency is commendable. Take some time to process your most recent expansion and rest in preparation for the next. Your evolvement is inspiring and the universe is applauding you.

Affirm

I am grateful for my growth.

29 September

Recognise that your expansion has heightened your sensitivities. Everything has become extremely enhanced from your vantage point. Your heart has opened to higher levels of awareness and can feel way more deeply with a broader scale of emotions. You may feel like your circumstances are being experienced by someone other than you, as you become accustomed to this new deeper scale of feelings now available. You may also feel like everything just got worse and be overwhelmed in unknown emotions about existing circumstances.

The process of your personal alignment to your highest truths requires that your heart opens to its fullest capacity. Your perception about your life and everything in it is shifting to higher levels of awareness where the complete dimensionality of love is felt in every circumstance. There's no more escaping all the love that you are. Feel it.

Affirm

I feel the new range of sensitivities available to me.

30 September

The cosmos is giving you the green light and the fuel for your journey. There are no restrictions or limitations to creating the life you want. However, the mind will locate subconscious data to try and convince you of why your desired route may not be plausible. Discernment is always necessary, even though fear and doubt have many different disguises; you're intelligent enough to not just skip off down any road because it may look appeasing.

It's time to trust and believe in yourself; nobody else can create or decide upon the life you want to live. Use this energetic green light to courageously move towards what your heart has been yearning for. The universe is waiting for your collaboration.

Affirm

I courageously step towards my heart's desires.

1 October

The need for external clarity and validation only drives you further away from yourself. The fact is you already know the truth, yet you're looking for others to confirm or contradict what is best for you. The subconscious may be seeking to confirm doubts and fears. You're only going to obtain the confidence needed to navigate your path if you trust yourself enough to keep taking steps without anybody validating or co-signing your every move. How much you trust yourself can be measured by how much you trust the universe.

Living your truth is an investment in yourself and demonstrates self-belief. You're gaining self-mastery when the opinion of others isn't needed or relevant to your journey.

Affirm

I am trusting myself more each day.

2 October

The veil has been broken and you're now able to see past the illusions. Epiphanies, aha moments, surprises and shocks are all examples of the dissolving veil. You've been trapped behind the veil living in a limited paradigm where Illusions have kept you stagnant and dormant. The veil has suppressed the truth, like the lie that should have never been told.

When your revelations reach you internally or externally, recognise and embrace the truths that have come to set you free. Accept that there are some things you could've never known or been made aware of until this moment. Trust in divine timing and alignments currently happening in your world.

Affirm

I accept and embrace the truths that are arriving.

3 October

Be observant of the energies that are around you. Is your spark of creativity being diminished by those who are unable to see things from your perspective? Are you feeling drained trying to convince everyone of the plausibility of your ideas? If the world was to overstand the creativity of every individual then there would be no original ideas or creations, only replication.

Seeking outside validation from others for your internal visions is similar to explaining to a blind person what the world actually looks like. Your creativity doesn't need approval, only your belief and confidence in yourself. Sometimes it's better not to share your vision in the early stages so that your creation can be formed without the doubt of outside influences. Let your creations do the talking.

Affirm

I embrace the original creative force that flows through me.

4 October

You are living in monumental times where you can be, do and have anything you want. You've been conditioned to believe you have no power and autonomy over your life when the opposite is true. This belief leaves you feeling hopeless and powerless over your own reality.

Gone are the days of being a victim of external circumstances. If you don't like something, say so. If you don't want to do something, don't. If you want to live a life less ordinary on the other side of the planet, do it. If you want to create something unfathomable, that defies all logic, do it. You can only change your reality if you own your truth in every moment in every way. Own your power of choice and honour what you really want in each moment: and reclaim the autonomy over your reality.

Affirm

I own the power of my free will, making choices that are aligned with my heart's truest desires.

5 October

There are several realities coexisting at the same time. Which one you will experience as your physical reality will depend upon what you've asserted your free will to choose. Free will is a gift and part of the human experience. The ability to predict future events has become unreliable due to you being a conscious creator and becoming aware of that ability and how to use it. Predictions will only relate to one of these possible timelines. Having an awareness about the details of a particular timeline can cause you to become attached to it and bring it into your reality, as your awareness and attachment subconsciously creates this reality by default.

You're a creationist and create momentarily: know you're capable of shifting timelines and creating new ones in an instant. Be mindful of what information you allow into your consciousness concerning your future. The desire to know routes and outcomes is best left unknown. You're going to get exactly where you need to be without a map and without directions. Your intuition is the only compass you'll need, authentically creating from your heart and soul.

Affirm

I consciously choose what timelines manifest without external influences and information.

6 October

Apply your wisdom and intuition to your current circumstances. This is not a time for procrastination in any form. You are fully equipped to make the necessary choices from the options that you are currently presented with. Your only hindrance is your doubt and lack of trust. Your insight and intuition sometimes need to be honoured through affirmative actions. This eliminates self-doubt and fears as your direct experiences will prove how illusionary your fears are once confronted with them.

New worlds are waiting to be explored, be courageous and do something you've never done before. The time is now.

Affirm

I have faith in my intuition and align my actions with my insights.

7 October

Your increasing levels of self-love are starting to manifest and will be reflected in your physical reality. You've done much internal work to align yourself with the love frequencies. Recognising that you are love has given you the ability to recognise love in all its various forms. Your increased love vibration like a magnet pulls to you all of the love, that you believe you are.

On your journey pay attention to when and how love shows up for you. Unconditional love is who you are in your purest form. Love is the energy that you're remembering to embody. Be prepared to be loved, unconditionally and unconventionally.

Affirm

I am magnetising all the love that I am to me.

8 October

Can you acknowledge what is right before your eyes? Every day is filled with blessings, are you aware of them? Opening your eyes this morning is a blessing, having air to breathe is a blessing, having the elements that sustain you and your sources of food, is a blessing. The universe feels your energy, are you expectant? Or are you grateful?

You are consistently surrounded by blessings in each moment. Practising gratitude and having an awareness of your blessings will allow you to acknowledge more blessings, and access more blessings. You're never blocked, limited or unfortunate, you're just unaware. Gratitude bestows endless blessings upon you. Acknowledge them.

Affirm

I acknowledge all of the blessings that surround me.

9 October

Gratitude needs to be woven into your consciousness, like a permanent state of mind or a consistent meditation in the background of your awareness. Gratitude is often forgotten when your focus is always directed towards achieving more, and being more. You want more evolvement, yet you're not grateful for your evolution thus far. You want to move yet you're not grateful that you have somewhere to live. You want a more abundant life yet fail to acknowledge the abundance that you're already blessed with.

Embodying the gratitude virtue requires constant practice of acknowledging, remembering and being grateful. Gratitude is a universal law that's always acknowledged. Align.

Affirm

I am constantly in a state of gratitude for my life.

10 October

Overcome your repetitive conditioned behaviours. Are you doing the same thing over and over again yet expecting different results? When you are repeating experiences there is still a blesson to be acquired. These reoccurring similar experiences have something to teach you, however you're not grasping the lessons necessary for your evolvement.

Past wounds have created beliefs that cause these conditioned robotic behaviours. Bring your awareness to the situation and choose a different behaviour. See the different paths and options currently available to you. Familiarity isn't always the best choice for your evolvement. Unknown paths and destinations is where you'll find the treasures.

Affirm

I consciously make new choices to assist my evolution.

11 October

Reflect on your life thus far, and think back to experiences that were painful and challenging. How did they turn out in the end? Where did you end up as a result of that challenging time? Has hindsight blessed you with the wisdom of those experiences? Now that you've evolved from those times, looking back you can now accept and acknowledge the benefit of what you had to go through, to be who you are now. Everything was divinely orchestrated to shape your life path. This process is continuous as you evolve.

As you reflect on your journey recognise that you can often experience challenging times, signalling that change is imminent. Although the intensity increases with each experience so does your ability to manage changes. Just like before you're supported by universal energies and there's higher plans you can't yet fathom. Use your strengths of your past experiences now, assimilating that you're capable, worthy and loved. Acknowledging that the universe is always supporting you.

Affirm

I utilise the wisdom of the past to assist my future.

12 October

Being responsible for your energy doesn't include feeling guilty about honouring what is right for you. Emotional manipulation tactics can surface when stepping into power and owning your truth. Your new-found authenticity intimidates those around you who are unable to show up for themselves in the same way. They fear losing you as they're struggling to overstand the new you.

Being authentic takes courage and owning your truth takes confidence. Both are cultivated through your belief and alignment to your higher self. Be wary of emotional situations that pull you away from your truth. Stay in alignment no matter how captivating the story seems.

Affirm

I honour what is right for me momentarily.

13 October

Overstand the dynamics pertaining to the new paradigms of life partner relationships. Gone are the days of relationships built around co-dependencies and needing somebody else to depend upon – to feel right, to be fulfilled, to help you, and to complete you. The dynamics surrounding relationships are shifting, and you may have already felt these rumblings in your personal life. The challenge, for you, is how to remain completely 100 per cent independently you, in your truth and authenticity, whilst being in a partnership? How do you not compromise, taint or dilute you when merging with your divine partner?

Find new ways of merging, explore sacred sexuality and tantra. Invite your spiritual selves into the divine union. Work on becoming more wholesome in your self-love and self-care and your experiences will become reflective of this. Traditionally structured partnerships are dissolving and being replaced with more authentic versions in alignment with the love you've been cultivating spiritually. Embrace these new energies, so humanity can raise the collective frequency of love.

Affirm

I maintain my independence and authenticity
when uniting in divine union.

14 October

Practise forgiveness with self, and others – it's time to heal and finally let go. You have undoubtedly faced and overcome many adversities on your journey. Yet these adversities still cling to you, as you cling to them. Practise self-forgiveness, you did what was best at that time with the information that was available to you. Hindsight is not there to make you feel guilty about past decisions and choices. Hindsight is where you gather awareness and wisdom from your experience.

Likewise with the others who formed part of that experience, they need forgiveness too. They're actors in your script of life on your stage, in your reality, assisting in your evolution process. They were contracted to form parts of your experience on Planet Earth. These agreements were made before your current incarnation and may even be a continuation of an agreement in a previous life. Whatever the circumstance, forgiveness is needed in order for you to release yourself from the bondage of the past. Every time you recall the wounded memory, forgive again.

Affirm

I forgive everyone who has been part of my evolution, including myself.

15 October

Realise your connection with all the forms of life on Planet Earth and the elements that sustain them. Quite often recognising that the air you breathe and the sun that shines is part of what sustains everyday life on Planet Earth, which enables you to be here and live.

Acknowledge all other life forms with the same love and respect that you acknowledge yourself with. Whether it's the plants and animals or what sustains them, they too are life, just as you are. When you connect with life energy in all forms you raise your own vibration and that of humanity's, increasing the consciousness of the planet. Go hug a tree, stroke a cat, and talk to the plants. They're waiting to connect.

Affirm

I connect with all the life forms on Planet Earth
with love and grace.

16 October

It's really easy to stay committed to the introverted lifestyle where all is fine and dandy in your bubble. There is a peace and comfort that exists in your own space which isn't as easily found in external spaces that are shared or belong to someone else. Your belief that your bubble keeps you safe from the world is an illusion when the world isn't even a threat to you. Alignment and evolvement require you to immerse yourself in the human experience.

Staying in your bubble, not interacting with the world, isn't challenging your consciousness or providing adequate openings for magic to occur. Step out fearlessly, confidently knowing that the world is waiting to receive you.

Affirm

I am stepping out of my comfort zone
confidently embracing the world.

17 October

There is so much more to your life than you can currently perceive, yet you've bound yourself so tightly to your current reality. Grasping tighter and tighter as the new becomes more visible and viable. Loosen your grip and remember all of the seeds that you've planted.

Don't lose yourself or your potential by being overly concerned with losing your current reality. What you perceive as loss is actually a gain. Trust the divine alchemy that is unfolding for your highest good. You're evolving and changing, losing all that is no longer needed. Know that any loss is always for your greater good, surrender with pride.

Affirm

I surrender to the blooming of the seeds I planted.

18 October

Being in the void is necessary for introspection. When your physical circumstances aren't reflecting the inner vision you'd hoped for you can become nonchalant, weary and unattached. Feeling as though you've exhausted all your options and that you've run out of ideas. Take a moment and pause from the outer reality that currently surrounds you. Go within and find your truths, and remember what they really feel like. Visualise them as if they already existed.

Remaining focused on your inner reality will be of greater benefit than fighting with your outer circumstances every day. Become like a chameleon who adapts to their physical environments instantaneously. Conserve your energy for being consistent with your truth and efforts, and this will sustain the vibration required to manifest your inner reality.

Affirm

I am focused on my inner reality and truths as
my life manifests effortlessly.

19 October

Step back and observe what is happening. You may feel as though you're stuck, when in fact it's a sign to slow down and look around. The feeling of being stuck by your physical reality serves as a space for you observe at a deeper level. Some circumstances can seem to be trapping and unfathomable. This is the time to take your focus away from the situation and physical reality. Turn your focus inward and listen to your intuition which provides great insights into your life. Being constantly embroiled in the physical momentum of your life, you can lose connection with your inner truths.

Spiritual expansion is required before physical manifestation can occur. Take some time out and go inwards for some deep introspection. What is being overlooked? What have you missed? What is beneath the surface, hidden from plain sight? Expand your awareness so that you can gain the clarity you need to move forward and carve the best path for you.

Affirm

I am observing my life and connecting to my intuition, noting all previous unknown aspects.

20 October

Release your need to be right. There is a difference between righteousness and consciousness, and being right is not always conscious. The knowingness that controls your life hinders your growth, as the unknown is the fertile seed that can grow into anything. Attachment to your perceived outcomes limits the possibilities of alternative results.

Pretending to know more than you actually do does not make you wise or bring you the wisdom you seek. Owning what you don't know will open you up to learning the same. It's okay not to know everything, that's where the mysteries of life are discovered, and magic unfolds. Embrace the uncertainty. You don't need to know everything or be right about anything. Authentically carve your path and make space for the magic to appear.

Affirm

I am a student of life forever, humble and open to learning.

21 October

Become aware of how much energy is being spent focusing on specific outcomes of various scenarios in your life. Attachment to obtaining desired results involves a continual projection and the need to control certain factors in your life. Whilst you are subconsciously behaving in this way, you lose much value from the actual experience of being present. Manifestation is influenced by your momentary thoughts, intentions and feelings. Being focused and attached to your desired outcome steals the present moments. Thinking that you'll be happy and fulfilled once you've achieved your desired goal(s) leaves this present moment empty and your happiness attached to a future outcome.

Decide to be happy now and to feel fulfilled in this present moment with exactly what you have now. Invest your energy in trusting your highest good. Become the observer, and always be grateful for constant change.

Affirm

I am happy and content in this present moment.

22 October

Overstand your presence on Planet Earth at this time, to be alive, now on the spiritual path to enlightenment is not a coincidence, whilst the ascension to higher consciousness is happening. Your personal journey of growth and development is part of the collective's rise of planetary consciousness. The work you have been diligently committed to doing is also serving the greater good of humanity's evolution.

You are fulfilling your soul purpose of assisting the ascension process just by being you and working on yourself, transcending your layers and trauma. The universe applauds and acknowledges all of your efforts you have made behind closed doors that nobody knows about. You truly are creating a new earth by recreating yourself.

Affirm

I am grateful I choose to be part of humanity's expansion into higher consciousness.

23 October

Love surrounds you in many forms. As you've learnt to love yourself on deeper levels your vibration is now emitting new higher frequencies of love. This means some things may no longer align with you and naturally dissipate, making room for what is in alignment with the new you. This energy will show up in various forms; try not to cling to your old story, deep transformation is occurring as the new you emerges.

Love life as life loves you, smell the flowers, talk to strangers, plants or animals, feel the sun on your face – and know it's a great time to be alive. Life loves you, in each and every moment, in every possible way.

Affirm

I am love and life loves me.

24 October

Become more consistent with your spiritual practices, so they become your daily disciplines. The journey of ascension requires that you learn how to stabilise and centre yourself, so that in times of turbulent energies and cosmic climates you have a toolkit to assist you. However, you'll have to use the tools for their levels of assistance to be taught to you. Knowledge of the tools without any regular practice is leaving you feeling abandoned, exhausted and overwhelmed.

Dig into your toolkit — find meditations that soothe your soul, spiritual baths that cleanse your aura and revitalise your spirit, time in nature to energise and heal you, foods that make you feel good, journaling to empty your heart and mind; and plenty of rest to integrate, stillness to calm the mind and listen to your intuition. Use your toolkit consistently for maximum benefits to help you gain your self-mastery.

Affirm

I use my spiritual toolkit to assist me.

25 October

You deeply desire change in your world yet you repress how you're feeling. Those around you are not mind readers and need to know how you feel to be able to support and assist you. Believing things will eventually sort themselves out helps you to ignore your own power to change your circumstances.

It's time to express yourself: find the confidence and courage to voice what is weighing on your heart and mind. If you don't like something, say so. Your opinions and feelings are valid and have a place in this world, claim it.

Affirm

I express my feelings knowing there is space for them to be received in the world.

26 October

Part of your journey is the consistent rebalancing of divine feminine, and divine masculine energies. As these energies start to harmonise and complement each other residual distortions are brought to the surface revealing to you unknown dissensions. Dominant forces from each of these energies have been conflicting and competing for many eons internally and externally.

As each rebalancing happens the reality about the truth of who you are shifts. Observe what comes up for you without attachments, recognising your own internal imbalances of masculine and feminine energies as they strive for unity within. Compassionately support your internal unification, knowing that you are whole and worthy of all that you deserve.

Affirm

I harmonise my masculine and feminine energies.

27 October

Restore some balance in your life. You may feel as though you're spinning a thousand plates at the same time, multitasking in every area of your life. This can make you feel ungrounded. Regain some order by being clear on what is a priority and what is not. Focus on what you can do and stop worrying about what you can't.

You can only do so much in one day and your time for you can't always be what is, compromised to fulfil the other areas of your life. Harmony has more value in your daily life than what can be completed in a day. Enjoy your journey, pace yourself and know that success will always be yours.

Affirm

I enjoy each day prioritising joy and my responsibilities equally.

28 October

Attribute your energy wisely. There is much outer chaos and distractions happening and ultimately, whatever you spend your energy on amplifies and becomes enhanced.

Before immersing yourself into any passing energies ask yourself, is this beneficial for me? Is this assisting humanity? Is this going to change my life? If the answers are no, why does it deserve any of your time?

This can appear to be selfish and single-minded; however this is necessary for your energy to be reserved for your path and your calling. Your energy and existence are precious; do not dissipate it on nothingness, invest it wisely.

Affirm

I intentionally invest my energy into beneficial situations.

29 October

The most important time is that of the energetic timelines that you're constantly expanding or collapsing. They create the grids for your future trajectories. You may have briefly sampled some of those frequencies through random windows as glimpses of the new are making themselves known through new random connections and possible opportunities.

Don't be overwhelmed with the intensity of what these glimpses show you; these are the openings to your new timelines. Much may still be quite unclear until the new timelines are completely installed. You've got much to look forward to in the new, take your time choosing what is right for you.

Affirm

I am patient in what I choose.

30 October

Recognise how you've been giving your power away, and how to reclaim it. You have your own connection to source and your own divinity, however you've been valuing and honouring external opinions like they know more about you, than you do. If you're consistently succumbing to what the external world has to say about your life, who's actually living your life?

Everyone needs a shoulder to cry on, a friend to confide in and a mentor to assist your growth. Learning to stay aligned with your truth in every interaction is to own your power and to know where you end and another begins. Have the confidence to trust yourself with your own opinion and truth. It's your truth that navigates the clearest path to your destination. Even when you feel you may have got it wrong, its right in the journey of your evolvement. Honour yourself first and reclaim your power.

Affirm

I am honouring my truth first in every moment.

31 October

Honour and acknowledge your personal cycles of death and rebirth. How many layers have you shed? How many times have you given birth to a higher version of you? Make peace with all that you've let go of, especially the previous versions of you that have died on your journey. Recognising that those deaths were necessary in your evolutionary process of re-birthing and revealing a more authentic you.

Be grateful, honour, respect and celebrate your constant resurrection, rebirth and renewal. You've come a long way, just take a look back and you'll see.

Affirm

I acknowledge my personal cycles of rebirth and renewal, I have grown immensely.

1 November

You're so consumed with being more you fail to recognise all that you've become and overcome. Your growth has been gradual yet consistent and some elements are not yet unrecognised by you. What used to trigger and irk you now doesn't even receive your attention or get absorbed into your consciousness anymore. Your connection with yourself has become much deeper and stronger, enabling you to navigate with more confidence in yourself and the universe.

Your growth has been epic. Applaud yourself, reflecting upon what stress used to look like and realising what it is now. Stop focusing on where you need to grow and recognise how much you've actually grown.

Affirm

I am evolving into higher consciousness and recognise my expansion.

2 November

You're unlearning who you believed yourself to be and replacing it with the truth of what you're actually discovering yourself to be. The process of discovery can be exhilarating as you assimilate the truth and disappointing at the same time. A lot of who you are was taught to you, and learnt throughout your life. Becoming aware of illusions that you've built your life upon can be heart-wrenching and take some time to fully accept.

The more you discover, the more authentic you can become. Don't judge how long it takes for you to apply your awareness to your reality. Be grateful that you have this awareness and let your intuition guide you.

Affirm

I am grateful that my awareness is expanding,
assisting me on my journey.

3 November

Magical energies surface when you can fully embrace uncertainty and the unknown. This demonstrates trust, faith and the ability to be in the flow with life. Submitting to a space of unpredictability means that you're ready to let go, release attachments and surrender to something greater than what currently exists.

Your soul provides all of the surety you need to stay safe in the unknown. Tune out of all the possibilities and probabilities. Accept that you're a divine soul destined for greatness whatever transpires.

Affirm

I embrace the unknown and the magic it holds.

4 November

Become more aware of the constant cycles of death and rebirth. In every moment you have an opportunity to birth a new aspect of self as you're given opportunities to choose new thoughts, feelings or actions. This process is a very conscious one and requires for you to be completely present with high levels of self-awareness. Aspects of you have been constantly dying and re-birthing anew your whole entire life. With maturity you've gained an awareness of these cycles and the adversities associated with them.

Establishing the authentic you requires conscious effort to be fully present in the physical reality, utilising the moments of opportunities when they arrive. Every time an old aspect dies, a new one is born. Keep evolving and choosing your truth in each and every moment. The new world is formed through you and by you.

Affirm

I am re-birthing anew in each moment.

5 November

You've become very accomplished at assessing your own damage limitations. Your evaluation of potential timelines is causing you to linger around, reluctant to make any moves. The internal debate can have you caught up in a quandary between wanting to take action, the perceived dangers and protecting yourself. Perceived dangers can incite unnecessary fears whereas a healthy awareness of potential risks and pitfalls maintain healthy caution.

Damage control has kept you confined to perceived fear-based limitations. Start solely focusing your evaluations and assessments on potential benefits, advantages and general goodness. Possibilities become realities: because you believe.

Affirm

I am able to see the positive opportunities that are available to me.

6 November

Your alchemy is required to balance your realities in alignment with the truth. As the new is being formed what you believe becomes more important than what you're physically experiencing. The physical reality is reflective of what was, what is and holds the seeds of potential for the future. Succumbing to the physical world with the belief that is all there is, and ever will be, dis-empowers and dis-engages your manifestation abilities. Holding your beliefs at the forefront regardless of what you're being presented with demonstrates how strong they are. These beliefs are shaped by your evolving truths.

The light of your truth is what creates new worlds. Is your belief and faith in your truths stronger than what you're physically experiencing?

Affirm

I have faith in my beliefs more than my physical reality.

7 November

You're encouraged to hold your faith and trust your own truths. Many will not be able to comprehend what you know to be true; your unique perception is for you to utilise whilst navigating your path. In order for you to fulfil your soul's contract, it's not relevant for anyone else to overstand your journey.

Your vision is as unique as you are; only you can implement what is needed to fulfil your vision. It's nice to have the support of your friends and family, however they may not be able to grasp the intricacies of your calling. Hold your light and your vision; manifest silently if need be; and let your achievements make the noise. Only you can do this.

Affirm

I trust my vision even when no one else can see it.

8 November

Much is recalibrating personally and universally causing heightened emotions and impulsive behaviours. You may be experiencing this personally or be receiving this energy from others. If you're experiencing this do some extra grounding work to strengthen your connection to Earth energies. If you are receiving this energy acknowledge it; however, choose not to react or respond to it. Do not allow it to trigger you into the same vibration. In either scenario take at least 30 seconds to check in with yourself before speaking or taking action on what you're being presented with. Disengaging from reactionary behaviours creates space for the awareness needed for clarity.

These unsettling energies are relative to the level of recalibration happening in other dimensions. Your physical world is being restructured in the other realms and this can make you feel dishevelled and anxious in the physical realm. Be patient with yourself, increase self-care and trust that all is well even though you can't see it yet.

Affirm

I ground myself into the Earth, embracing my recalibration.

9 November

Your evolvement is bringing you into alignment with your vortex. You have shed many layers and matured in your perceptions of self and Planet Earth. This brings about the alignment with the truth of who you really are. Regardless of what is showing up in your reality, it's imperative to stay focused on your internal reality and creationist abilities. It's your beliefs that are shaping the new world.

Be patient with your physical reality and allow the universe to co-create magic with you. All you need to do is hold the vision and believe. The new world is being created by you and through you. Envision the truth you wish to see.

Affirm

I am patient with my physical reality and focused on my internal vision and truth.

10 November

The energy of limitless possibilities surrounds you. Whatever your current vision and dreams are expand them × 1,000,000%; that's the type of manifestation powers available in these current energies. Expand your dreams and visions way beyond your current perceived limitations. This is not the time to be shrinking to fit the apparent circumstances. Dare to dream big and believe it.

Your unique message and imprint are channelled through your specific ambitions, desires, and dreams. It is up to you to have the courage and confidence to align your physical actions with your internal vision. This is the time to believe in yourself and know that your personal vision is plugged into the grander vision of the new Earth template. Your level of self-belief is what manifests the world around you. Hold the grandest vision you can find and believe it, for the universe is supporting you and humanity depends on you.

Affirm

I envisage my biggest, most impossible dreams with the belief they can make manifest.

11 November

Higher frequency vibes are available today as you're bathed in waves of photonic light. The frequencies and vibrations that you can feel are a sample of what higher consciousness feels like. This is the permanent vibration that you're expanding into and becoming, the destination to where we're all headed. Portals like this are a sneak peek at the energetic vibrations you're starting to encompass and the levels of consciousness you've reached.

Spend time connecting to and being in the awesome high frequencies that surround you today. Know that this is just a taste of what is to come and is available to you because you've been doing the work. This is what alignment feels like. Enjoy.

Affirm

I am receiving all the light codes and higher frequencies available to me.

12 November

The influx of light currently being channelled to Earth and her inhabitants may be causing any residual energies from your intense healing journey to surface. You may be basking in and embodying the wave of incoming higher light frequencies or experiencing physical ascension symptoms. This can make you feel distraught and frustrated with challenges and old emotions appearing.

What you may experience as a result of being bathed in this light is dependent upon where your soul is in its journey. If you're feeling overcome with darkness or denseness this is the overwhelming light pushing everything to the surface in any form it can. Self-care is key to navigating these portals and embracing this as another phase to your evolvement process.

Affirm

I am riding the waves of evolvement and the highs and lows on my journey to enlightenment.

13 November

You may have become emotionally overwhelmed with the influx of new energies, crying to release deep buried grief, trauma and adversities. The solar plexus and heart chakras have been cracked open. Anything unhealed or unresolved has been exposed to the light and brought to the surface for clearing, through your tears; clearing the cellular memories from your body that hold unnecessary subconscious data. You're transcending for your entire bloodline and may not have full awareness of what is stored in your DNA.

Cry until you can't cry anymore, that's how you know you've felt the full spectrum of trapped emotions and transcended them. Crying is an extremely powerful cleansing and healing tool that removes the debris in a way which allows you to feel the intensity of your own pain and safely release it. Embrace your tears as they cleanse your soul.

Affirm

I release all trauma from my DNA.

14 November

The universe is very apt at finding new ways to usher you into your desired timeline. This can become very tedious work when your desires change every time you feel you can't have what you want. You're so easily dismayed when the physical world isn't conducive to your desires, that you'll change or shrink your desires to fit in with what's currently available.

Stay committed to your vibrational frequency, consistently honouring what you want and know to be possible. Don't compromise or falter when doubtful influences arrive. You can be, do and have what you want if you dare to believe in yourself and trust the universe. Dismiss anything that's not for you.

Affirm

I am committed to my vision and truth.

15 November

In the space in-between the dismantling of the old and building of the new there's a pregnant pause, filled with infinite potential and the seedlings of your dreams and desires. Mass clearings have taken place on many levels internally and externally. This is a powerful shift that you've been waiting for.

Embrace the meantime knowing there is a physical manifestation of the spiritual, emotional and mental work you've been doing. Use this meantime to rest, rejuvenate and integrate. When you've been doing the work in all the other areas of your life, you'll see the magic of your co-creation with spirit unfold effortlessly.

Affirm

I embrace the meantime. Resting and restoring
in preparation for the next phase.

16 November

Establishing the new world and your evolving vibration relies on your ability to speak and act upon your truths. The truths which you're most fearful to share and act upon are the truths that create new paradigms and build new worlds. Suppressing your truth because you fear how it may be received and impact others suppresses you and your expansion, dimming your light in the process.

Speaking and acting in alignment with your personal truths demonstrates how authentic you're prepared to show up in the world. The old world, like the new, only exists with your contribution, input, and belief. Which world are you contributing to?

Affirm

I am contributing to the new world through acting in alignment with my truth.

17 November

Take some time out and rest, pushing ahead will not bring the answers that you're seeking. There have been huge light influxes and you're shifting internally as the light code updates are integrating. Feeling overwhelmed, indecisive, confused and empty all at the same time is part of the integration process. This, coupled with random ascension symptoms, can leave you feeling quite fraught.

The answers come when you are still and at peace. Rest and self-care are the only ways to navigate this corridor. You will find the pot of gold at the end of the rainbow. Allowing yourself the space to be, relax and unwind, will give you the bird's eye view you've been seeking. Breathe, spend time in nature and eat nature's foods, aligning yourself with the rainbow light, locating your pot of gold.

Affirm

I am still resting and nurturing myself through
the integration process.

18 November

Reset your assistance vibration by requesting what you need. There are many areas of your life where you would like expansion to occur; however, realise that mulling it over in your mind hasn't given you what you need. Now it's time to call in the higher energies that you're connected to. Your angels, spirit, ancestors and guides are all waiting patiently for your invitation to intervene on your behalf. Contrary to what you may believe you're not alone, you're supported by divine beings and universal energies. However, they require invitations to keep showing up for you.

Start a new practice of connecting with the divine energies that surround you daily. You'll be amazed at how quickly your life expands with universal assistance.

Affirm

I invite the higher energies to assist my evolution.

19 November

You may be feeling the pressure to make decisions. When you become overwhelmed with your feelings and your emotions are running high, making a choice seems like the only way to regain some type of control over your world.

Be patient and observe what is currently happening without attachments. These observations will prove useful in the near future. All of the details and necessary data have not yet been presented to you. The remaining relevant information will be available for you to perceive very soon. You'll then be able to make informed decisions once all the factors are on the table. For now, just kick back, relax and rest until it's time to make choices and take action.

Affirm

I make informed decisions without feeling pressured.

20 November

With growth and expansion comes an increased responsibility for your energy. Time has sped up, quickening the processes of evolution. Growth which used to take months is now happening in moments. This can be exhausting, rapidly consuming your energy reserves, leaving you depleted and lethargic.

You have all the tools needed to balance, restore and boost your energy. Double and triple your investment into your practices and disciplines if necessary. Increased awareness enables you to be more responsible for your energy, demonstrating that you're prepared to progress to the next stage of your evolvement. Time to level up.

Affirm

I balance and replenish my energies with my spiritual practices.

21 November

Connect with your ancestors and lineage. If you don't have a regular practice of connecting with those gone before, now is a good time to start. Honouring your ancestors is also honouring yourself, acknowledge and respect those that made it possible for you to be here now. You have the genetics of 2,400 of your ancestors encoded into your DNA. You have access to all of their traits, gifts and achievements and can be anything they were and more.

Your ancestors' energy is always very present around you and within you. Make offerings of thanks for their existence, assistance and giving you life today. You are because they were. The legacy continues.

Affirm

I connect with my ancestors and all the magical power in my DNA.

22 November

You can only perceive what is available for you to process. Current perceived obstacles are likely to disappear with new intel. This new information is probably the catalyst for change that you've been waiting for. You're being awoken to your new way of being in the new world. Being enlightened with new intelligence creates access to higher perspectives, revealing more new aligned paths for you to explore.

The metamorphosis can be rough or smooth dependant on your ability to stabilise yourself in a storm. The agenda is change, evolution and growth. Don't get engulfed by the tides of truth arriving to usher in your transformation.

Affirm

I accept and embrace the truth that ushers in my evolution.

23 November

For the new to be established, you'll have to try new things. The new needs your participation to exist and come into physical form. The new isn't going to be created if you continue doing what you've always done. Familiarity doesn't challenge your consciousness enough to incite evolutionary changes. Be innovative: try new things that spark your passion: travel on unknown routes and discover new ways of being and relating.

Engaging in new activities, new people and new places will give you the experience needed to decide what paths you'd like to explore further. Enjoy exploring the unlimited newness.

Affirm

I am engaging in new experiences and exploring life.

24 November

The universe offers you an opportunity to set new intentions in alignment with the new you. Much of what you believed to be true has been dismantled, and what you want keeps evolving. Every time you shed a layer and shatter an illusion new perspectives are born, providing you with greater vantage points and breaking perceived limitations. Become comfortable in setting new intentions with your new perspectives even if that is subject to change.

What's important is that you utilise this present moment and harness what your desires are, in the moment of now. Ensure that your intentions are always aligned with your current desires to keep expanding the manifestation of the new world.

Affirm

I am revising my intentions with my enhanced perspectives.

25 November

Recognise and acknowledge the fertility of the new soil you have cultivated. The transcendence of much toxicity internally and externally has cultivated very fertile grounds for you, in every area of your life. This fertility requires you to be in a centred space with your intentions rooted in wholeness. Ensuring your choices are coming from a place of worthiness, self-love and overall wellbeing.

Overstand that prior blockages and all imbalances have now been transcended. What was, no longer is. You're free to be your wholesome self, knowing that you're deserving of all the abundance in the multiverses.

Affirm

My intentions are rooted in the wholeness of my entire being.

26 November

Become more aware of the people that you have attracted into your life. Your vibe will always attract your tribe. Many of them bring blessons to you and have an impact on your evolvement. Look for those who bring out the best in you and challenge you to be better. Some will assist you in your adversities, whilst others may create adversities. Either way there is a blesson to be learnt from the experience.

The universe creates circumstances and people that cause you to level up. Be grateful for these influences that continuously show up to expand your awareness and test and create your virtues. There some influences causing you to reflect, pay attention to them. For they come as catalysts for your growth and evolvement: leading you to higher planes.

Affirm

I am aware of the experiences and people that I have attracted into my life.

27 November

Honour how you feel. Your life is about your happiness and contentment, you don't owe anybody anything. If you just want to curl up on the sofa and do nothing, you can, you're allowed. Honouring yourself defines new paradigms and creates new timelines. You can change your mind as often as you feel it's necessary to stay in alignment with self. Engaging with what you know is not aligned with you, only brings you farther out of alignment the longer you continue to engage with it.

Energies are supporting self-love and staying aligned with your truths. Make sure you're content, happy and aligned to maintain harmonious vibrations.

Affirm

I honour my feelings in each moment.

28 November

Your evolution is guaranteed once you've incarnated into this physical realm. Your evolution has demonstrated that your next timeline is always more aligned then the previous one. The cycles of growth are obvious and self-evident, reflecting the areas of growth with each expansion.

Things aren't the same because you're not the same. Your vibration has changed, and you've matured in many aspects. What's laid before you is another reflection of your growth and expansion. Take your uniquely crafted path and walk in your purpose, trusting the work is done.

Affirm

I own my new vibration and walk my path confidently.

29 November

Embrace the meantime. As you step out of the old into the new there's a void of desolate emptiness. A place where it feels as though nothing exists; the old is dissipated and the new not yet formed. Realise that neither world, the past nor future exist right now in this present moment.

Utilize these precious moments to be present with yourself right here, right now. Embracing uncertainty as you're assimilating the new. Be certain that you can trust yourself in this present moment, knowing all that you've become.

Affirm

I embrace the meantime, being present in this moment.

30 November

Learn to practise humility more often. Recognise that there are times to be assertive and times to step back. Start to acknowledge what may be more appropriate for you, and when. Stepping back from centre stage allows you to see what else is actually on the stage and how you can better place yourself and cast roles. Gathering virtues is part of becoming enlightened, humility is just one of them.

Remain grounded in your truth and focus on mastering yourself. Stop rushing to do too much too soon, you will become who you're going to be regardless if you walk, run, hop or skip. Utilise the power of humility on your journey, it has many gifts.

Affirm

I humble myself gaining the clarity I need.

1 December

Go and experiment with your new vibration. It has been quite a dense few months and you've done a lot of work on many levels, most of which cannot be seen with the physical eye. The deep inner work that you have been doing has led to much isolation and solitude. However, human connection is a vital part of your journey and growth. To hold space when you need, being your reflection, sharing your journey and being the channel for spirit when there's something you need to know.

Prolonged introverted behaviour can make you feel alone and lonely out here. Too much solitude can spiral you into negative thinking. Embrace a new season, reach for your 'glad rags' and know that hibernation is over. Time to go explore the new you, in the physical realm, with others just like you.

Affirm

I am ready to explore the outside world with my new vibration.

2 December

Become more aware of your ESP (extrasensory perception) which is your 6th senses. Whether it's telepathy, astral travelling, being psychic, remote viewing, clairvoyance, etc., having senses outside of the 3rd dimension physical realm can take some getting used to. There's a plethora of ESP abilities that are accessible to you; natural curiosities and passions will decide which ones you'll develop along the way.

Everyone is intuitive and has intuition, which is the foundation to all of the six senses working with you, and for you. Learning to listen to your insights and aligning your physical world with your intuitive world is part of anchoring higher consciousness into the physical realms. Through conditioning and habitual behaviours you can forget your 6th senses exist and get locked into 3D matrix. This may be momentarily, or for days, weeks or months. The ability to maintain connections with your 6th senses and live in a 3D world is a skill that you must learn and acquire to navigate your path and bring higher consciousness to the physical plane. Alignment with higher dimensional consciousness whilst in physical form is ascension.

Affirm

I am aware of my ESP and gifts that are accessible to me, in my journey.

3 December

Your expansion has been tremendous. You've transformed into a unique butterfly after spending months being cocooned; it's time to fly and share your beauty with the world. A lot has been released in your healing process. Your cocoon of transformation has now gone, taking with it all that was revealed inside.

Your focus now is to remain in high frequencies by being happy, joyful, content and grateful; you stay in alignment with your vortex. Whatever is defined in your vortex will manifest more easily as you maintain your higher vibrations. The universe applauds your transformation.

Affirm

I am flying high, grateful, happy and in awe of my journey.

4 December

Clear yourself internally and externally from any unnecessary debris and clutter. Whilst walking the path you've attained many things which were once purposeful and useful in your world. You've also accumulated a library of memories and experiences, some of which still hold a resonance and emotional charge, whether positive or negative.

It's time to clean house and let go of those things that serve no purpose and have no future use. You don't want to keep being pulled back into the past once you're moving forwards. Tie up any loose ends or unfinished business and make space for the new.

Affirm

I release all attachments to anything not serving my highest good.

5 December

The new doesn't just encourage you to be your authentic self, it forces the manifestation of that expression. Who you are is not what you articulate it to be, it's what you actually do in every moment. That is the expression of the authentic self. If your actions are not aligned with your hypotheses of who you believe yourself to be, circumstances and situations will occur for you to demonstrate what that is. Your actions prove who you are and will either align with your beliefs and ideals about yourself or not. Ingrained behaviours can cause you to act from your old beliefs.

The new is here for those who can implement their new behaviours and beliefs. Until then, it's Groundhog Day with more of the same. Applying what you know to be true is how you step into your new timelines that are waiting for you to align. Claim your autonomy in your life.

Affirm

I am in alignment with my beliefs and demonstrate my truths.

6 December

You can be, do and have what you want. You've been conditioned to believe that being successful and abundant is something only the privileged or the 'lucky' can achieve or acquire. After living with this belief for so long, you've excluded yourself from knowing your true worthiness and potential.

The impossible is made possible, initially by your belief that it is possible and actions that confirm that belief. The universe responds to your vibration and can only deliver what you allow, and are open to receiving. Utilise the powerful manifestation energies available. What you want is wanting you, know what that is and align.

Affirm

I am worthy of receiving the abundance of the universes.

7 December

Your consciousness is expanding rapidly and the embodiment of these higher dimensions requires for you to fully trust your new-found levels of spiritual awareness, especially when nothing looks or feels the same. You're only feeling stuck because you're unsure of what to do. Don't let the fear creep in and start doubting or second guessing what you're feeling because you're in new territories. Your upgrade and expansion have aligned you with more of your spiritual awareness and gifts. You're learning to become more reliant on them as you navigate the higher frequencies.

Your faith and trust that has navigated you thus far continue to trail blaze just like you've been doing. The new world is beckoning; you'll find it in everything that you're afraid to do.

Affirm

I trust the intel my awareness provides, assisting me to navigate my path.

8 December

Linear time constructs are fading and your time concepts are shifting. The momentum of time is changing as you vibrate higher and become less concerned with it. When you do check the time you notice how slowly or quickly it has passed in comparison to your internal clock. Eating and sleeping no longer happen at the designated times. Eating happens when you're hungry, even if that's in the middle of the night. Sleeping happens when your physically tired not because its night time. You may have noticed that you need less of both. Your body is reassigning your sources of energy as you evolve into more crystalline frequencies.

This evolution of time is aligning you with many new frequencies, effortlessly, as you focus more on being here now. Expect alignments, magic, and miraculous events as you experience more of this new time space.

Affirm

I create my own perception of time and live by my own clock.

9 December

It's time to take a break and give yourself a much needed rest: your light body has been doing much integration work after all the light code updates to your DNA. You're putting extra stress on yourself by trying to force physical manifestations to happen now. Cajoling is a complete waste of your energy at this point, nothing happens before its time.

Have faith that you're doing the necessary work to attain your desires. Invest your energy into something else that will engage your mind. Have a massage, go for a hike, make something creative, just do something other than what you've been doing. Much magic can happen when we take our focus away from our immediate physical lives. Disengage from your stresses and woes; instead choose to engage with the beautiful moments that constantly surround you.

Affirm

I am relaxing and enjoying the now, as I integrate more light.

10 December

Utilise the power of your imagination and creativity. In times of change and recalibration, when nothing is certain and the unknown lurks in every corner, your imagination can provide the stability and certainty you need. The concepts visualised in this realm can be more real and fluid than your physical reality. It allows you to detach from the chaos and connect with potential timelines that exist. Spending time envisioning and imagining all the potential scenarios you could be immersed in is a worthy investment. It will assist you in finding the timeline that is most suitable and manifesting it into your physical reality.

Daydreaming is an extremely important part of knowing and manifesting the life you want. Sneak previews are now being shown through your imagination; tune in to see yours. Escape the illusion of your reality.

Affirm

I utilise my imagination to envisage potential timelines and realities I would like to experience.

11 December

Increase your boundaries, your expansion requires for you to be more responsible with your energy. As you evolve boundaries have to be established and enforced for you to protect your energy. How you use your energy and whom you share it with determines your level of responsibility. As you vibrate higher, you will receive tests in the form of your old story. Pay attention to those that adhere to your boundaries and those that try to continuously compromise them. Release that which is not aligning with your vibration.

Everything is not worthy of your energy, time and focus. When you realise that you're a spiritual warrior on a divine mission, you'll recognise how many things that are distractive to your path. Be responsible and purposeful with your energy. To acquire more of your power, you'll have to demonstrate you can manage what you already have, responsibly.

Affirm

I am establishing boundaries and protecting my energy.

12 December

Focus on self-care and rest as intense surges of light are streaming to Planet Earth and her inhabitants. This will be felt in resonance with where you are in your journey. Hidden emotions and feelings may surface as the light code updates integrate and flush out any lower frequency dense matter. You already hold awareness about what is surfacing as you believed you'd already healed and transcended these feelings. Or you may be having a totally contrasting experience, feeling high vibratory influxes and riding the cosmic waves to your benefit.

However this is showing up in your world, allow yourself to feel what is currently moving through you without judgement or attachments. Increase self-care to soothe the intensity of what you're experiencing. Take it easy, slow down the pace and allow yourself to recalibrate through to the solstice.

Affirm

I am resting, recalibrating and embracing the influxes of light.

13 December

Take some time out for yourself. In amongst the seasonal commitments, consumerism and festive celebrations, recognise that you're in an intense solstice portal that has magical manifestation energies available to you.

If you've been focusing on particular timelines or desires this year now is the time to revisit those visualizations and intentions. The dreamy sleepy energy you feel is the incubation stage required for growth and transformation. In the same way camera film negatives go to the lab to be processed and developed you too need processing and developing time. Enjoy some much needed time out.

Affirm

I am taking time out to process and develop my expansion.

14 December

As old timelines collapse and you release the old story you may be experiencing emotional and physical pains together with life changing events. Or you are logging onto the possible new timelines, being filled with excitement and joy, contemplating the newness. Whatever you're experiencing at the moment is right for you and your evolvement. The levels of disturbance you may be feeling are related to your attachments, fears, self-worth and nostalgia. The old story has a lot of attachments and took you a lifetime to build.

This is the completion of old looping timelines and cycles that have blocked your expansion. The new can only be formed if the old is completely dismantled; surrender and embrace your transformation.

Affirm

I accept the process of my transformation.

15 December

The planet and her inhabitants are receiving activations, accessing higher consciousness. Low frequency energies will tussle to keep you entrapped in the belief that your desires, dreams and future aspirations are unattainable. New tactics and cunning schemes are deployed, testing your resilience, faith and commitment. If you've learnt how to stay in your truth and have faith in your beliefs, you will be able to coast through. If you doubt what you believe, your fears will be met in your experiences.

You've become a master at overcoming and transcending lower vibrations; don't allow any trickster circumstance to take away the power of your truth. Own your vibration, now more than ever. Your truth is the light.

Affirm

I own my truth, power and light.

16 December

Amazing high-frequency energies are currently available to you. Tune in to these awesome frequencies, as this is a glimpse of what is to come, living in higher consciousness. Being in the physical world and yet not attached to it, almost as if you're floating above your own reality. You'll be able to see everything with an eagle's view, with the highest perception and universal wisdom. Manifestation can be instantaneous in these higher frequencies. Be mindful of your thoughts and words or use them constructively, to manifest exactly what you want.

You're being bathed in this potent golden light and held in higher frequencies, which are available to everyone. Enjoy your short exploration and experimentation in this burst of higher consciousness. It's a real glimpse of the new world and the efforts of collective consciousness.

Affirm

I am embodying all the higher frequencies available to me.

17 December

You're surrounded by creative energies. You may have previously received insights about new projects, or just random insights, with various ideas that never manifested in the physical realm. All of those creative insights are now coming together, to form a solid vision of how to physically manifest an entire ideal.

This may not be what you had in mind, or what you had previously envisaged yourself to be drawn to. The pieces of the puzzle are finally coming together; you're now able to see the path that leads to your individual destination. You're being called to build the new world, your world.

Affirm

I am putting the pieces of the puzzle together, building the new world.

18 December

Be grateful for your choices. Each choice you've made has led you to being who you are now, where you are now. You choose to walk a particular path that you never knew would, or could, lead to now. Even in the moments of challenges and adversities, you've been able to accept them as catalysts and support to your growth. You're learning how easy it is to choose again once you've outgrown your previous choice; overstanding that loyalty and devotion are only required for choices that are supportive of your evolution.

Even when you felt you made a bad choice in hindsight, you can see how good it really was. You did this – your courage, your determination and your navigation. Don't doubt your skills or your ability to be aligned, in the right place at the right time. Trust yourself.

Affirm

I am aligning more with each choice I make.

19 December

Be prepared to receive love in many forms. Your love frequency has increased as you're learning to love yourself more and more each day, your love vibration expands and heightens. You've become more aware of the love that surrounds you and have naturally become more grateful. When your gratitude vibration expands, so does your ability to receive more.

The domino effect is at work in your world from self-love, to gratitude, to love and back. Expect to find love in unexpected places, people and things. Love comes in various forms, many of which you're still to discover. Unconventional love will be finding you everywhere and anywhere.

Affirm

Life loves me in each and every moment, in every possible way.

20 December

There's a reset in process. You have been taking one step forwards and two steps backwards for most of this year. No more treading water and reaching nowhere. This year has been invaluable in demonstrating how to decipher and recognise what you really want and need. Your internal accuracy is now well defined and re-aligned with your highest path.

Take some time to acknowledge your progress and growth. Lingering self-doubt has been transmuted into security and self-confidence. You've done some awesome work and moved mountains to get here. Go celebrate your achievements and clarity.

Affirm

I am moving forward, with clarity and faith in my journey.

21 December

Follow your intuitive desires. Powerful manifestation energies abound, supporting the physical creation of new personal timelines, woven into the elevation of collective consciousness and humanity's ascension process. Don't try to ignore or deny your instinctive urges; acknowledging the heart message maintains your vibration and alignment.

You're being ushered to open new doors that will align with your new timelines. Some doors may require the special keys of wisdom you hold to open them. Don't look for the logic or common sense in where or what your intuition is guiding you towards now; magic is not linear.

Affirm

I am acknowledging the messages from my soul,
opening new doors with my wisdom.

22 December

Be more considerate and compassionate towards others. Everyone is a product of their environment, and some have little consciousness and awareness of self. When someone is not exposed to a vast range of knowledge, skills and behaviours their perceptions can become limited to what they do know. It's not ignorance or arrogance; some people don't get it because they really can't grasp the concept. Psychological and emotional intelligence is required to be able to process information and communicate effectively.

Be patient and take time to listen; and extend your empathy and compassion to know why this exists instead of condemning its existence. You can probably identify with being this person now or sometime throughout your journey. Never forget that you had a process to your growth and evolution. Share your love even when it's incomprehensible.

Affirm

I am compassionate towards all souls on their journey.

23 December

Your growth is meritorious. The culmination of all the energy you have been investing in healing and transcending your wounds is dissolving the patterns and cycles that have been present for most of the year. You have attained new levels of self-awareness, perceiving the contributory factors to your growth and wisdom that made you.

Your connection to source and light has increased. You have become more illuminated and this will be reflected in your physical world. You're doing incredible things for yourself and humanity. Keep going, the world needs you and spirit sees you.

Affirm

I am grateful for my expansion.

24 December

Applaud your ability to tune into your soul, adhere to your intuition, and delve into feeling your pain. You may feel as though your efforts have gone unnoticed; this is not true. The universe has been supporting and watching your every move, with or without your awareness. Your ability to navigate the constant turbulence is becoming very masterful. You're learning how easy it is, to be a spiritual human being, accepting yourself more and allowing all aspects their rightful place in your life.

Humanity is ascending as a faster pace because of your discipline; loyalty and commitment to your path. You're fulfilling your potential in this lifetime, even though at times it may not seem like it. The portal of light you are shines brightly through into the multiverses. You're forever visible like the star you are, making an impact with every twinkle.

Affirm

I am committed to my growth and evolution.

25 December

You can create new traditions to replace the old. It is traditional for many to partake to habitual celebrations on this day every year. Many have broken away from the religious celebrations and the biblical birth of Jesus Christ. Ponder for a moment what does today mean for you? What are you celebrating? Are you doing what you've always done because it is the norm or what is expected of you? Are you present in Christmas energy intentionally or habitually? Be aware of your own reasons and intentions before investing your energy into anything.

In this time of seasonal celebrations take a moment to send love to those who have no shelter, no food and no loved ones to care. Acknowledge that Christ Consciousness has been accessible for some time now and is available for all those who choose it. Soul wishes you a merry everything and to be happy always.

Affirm

I am intentionally investing my energy into what I desire.

26 December

Settling for mediocrity when you're destined for greatness blocks your blessings. When your desires don't show up in time, you can lose faith and choose something else instead. The something else isn't quite what you wanted; however, you're happy to make do. Constantly compromising your desires demonstrates that you have little faith and belief in the manifestation of them. If you baked bread without yeast, it wouldn't rise. Trust, faith and belief are necessary parts of the alchemical recipe needed for manifestation.

The universe does not interfere in free will. You'll never get what you want if you're always accepting alternatives. If you want coffee, don't accept the tea when it's offered. Your soul has deeper yearnings; align with your choices, belief, faith and inner knowing that all things are possible.

Affirm

I am accepting nothing less than what I truly want.

27 December

As you step into your new timelines and onto your new trajectory, you will be presented with new obstacles and challenges. Stepping into your greatness means that you're powerful enough to overcome whatever you're presented with. Every level presents a different devil and demands that you own your greatness in order to overcome. Don't be dismayed if you're presented with things you had no prior knowledge or consideration of. These things have only surfaced and become visible because you've stepped into higher timelines.

Acceptance is key to navigating into next year and will assist you in finding your resolve, whatever you're presented with. You're more powerful than you believe and aligned with the universe more than you know. Own your greatness and your new timelines.

Affirm

I am accepting what surfaces as part of my evolution process.

28 December

You've made it through another ride on the ascension roller coaster and are well on the path to enlightenment. The experiences on your journey are the teachers for acquiring your virtues. Access to your gifts and power are given once you've obtained your virtues, providing the necessary responsibility for your potential power. Reflect on your growth, what virtues you have gained and how much you've matured.

Take some rest now, the New Year guarantees faster rides, accessing more of your gifts, enlightenment, power and self-mastery. You won't need to buckle up either, as you've learnt some amazing navigation skills on your awe-inspiring journey, continuously confirming your capabilities every step of the way.

Affirm

I am inspired by my own growth.

29 December

Your expansion has allowed you to encompass so much. You're now more aware of where you end and another begins. What used to trigger you, now bounces off of you. What used to enrage you is now more subtlety received. All of the energy you've invested into becoming the authentic you and every microscopic change you've embodied, has contributed to the ascension of planetary and collective consciousness.

Your evolution is continuously in progress and you're well on your way on the Ascension Highway. Take regular moments to pause, breathe and realise all that you've become. The growth you've achieved is quite significant, and the universe is extremely proud of your contributions.

Affirm

I am embodying more of my authenticity each step of the way.

30 December

Even though you're in the time of year when everyday feels like Sunday, a lot is happening in the other realms, which is in the process of manifesting into your physical reality. What occurs in the higher dimensions always manifests physically as an end result.

You've been doing the work spiritually, and you're now having an intense integration, upgrade and clearing. Whatever your current experience is, whether sombre or dramatic, this is part of what is needed before your next physical expansion. Trust the process, you're right on time.

Affirm

I embrace my experiences in the next stage of my expansion.

31 December

There's much to take in when you reflect upon your journey this year and this entire decade. You've achieved a lot and evolved immensity. You've gained so much wisdom through your experiences and you'll be moving forward with ease. At this stage in your evolvement very little can elude your awareness.

It's time to show yourself some gratitude and appreciation amongst your reflection. It was you who navigated yourself to your current trajectory. You've turned adversities into wisdom: it's you who applied knowledge and wisdom to facilitate change personally and collectively. Really appreciate who you are and who you've become, in this monumental time of ascension. Happy new conscious moments, value your time and invest it wisely.

Affirm

I am thankful for my journey and who I am becoming.